Administration

3rd edition

NVQ LEVEL 1

Carol Carysforth
Mike Neild

Student handbook

Heinemann

Heinemann Educational Publishers,
Halley Court, Jordan Hill, Oxford OX2 8EJ
A division of Reed Educational & Professional Publishing Ltd

Heinemann is a registered trademark of
Reed Educational & Professional Publishing Limited

OXFORD MELBOURNE AUCKLAND
JOHANNESBURG BLANTYRE GABORONE
IBADAN PORTSMOUTH NH (USA) CHICAGO

First published 2002
2006 2005 2004 2003 2002
10 9 8 7 6 5 4 3 2 1

A catalogue record for this book is available from
the British Library on request.

ISBN 0 435 45168 5

Typeset by 🔺 Tek-Art, Croydon, Surrey

Printed and bound in Great Britain by The Bath Press Ltd, Bath

Tel: 01865 888058 www.heinemann.co.uk

Contents

SPECIAL NOTE

Guidance on the following skills is freely available on the Heinemann
website at www.heinemann.co.uk/vocational/NVQ password
ADMINSKILLS): Improving your writing skills; Improving your number
skills; Your rights and responsibilities at work.

Council for Administration

This NVQ/SVQ publication is based on the national occupational standards developed by the Council for Administration (CfA), which is the Government-approved body representing the sector of Administration. Copyright of the national occupational standards is the property of the CfA and, as such, the standards may not be reproduced or transmitted in any form or by any means without written permission from the CfA.

For further information on the work of the CfA, including the Administration Standards, please contact:

The CfA
18/20 Bromell's Road
London SW4 0BG
Telephone: 020 7627 9876
Fax: 020 7627 9877
Email: **nto@cfa.uk.com**
Website: **www.cfa.uk.com**

Introduction to NVQ Administration

This section gives you important information on your NVQ Administration award. It also tells you how this book has been designed to help you with both your NVQ and your Key Skills, if you are also taking Key Skills units.

Understanding NVQ awards

NVQ awards are quite different from other types of qualifications, such as GCSEs. They are designed to help you to achieve the skills you need at work, and a variety of NVQs are available for people who want to work in a range of jobs, such as retailing, catering, hairdressing and so on. You have chosen to do an NVQ in Administration which means you are interested in working in an office – or already work in one – and want to learn and develop the skills you need in this area.

There are different levels of NVQs. Level 1 is the first level for Administrators and level 5 the top level – for very Senior Administrators. Therefore, if you enjoy doing your NVQ and want to progress, a natural step would be to do NVQ 2 Administration next.

NVQ units

Every NVQ has a number of **units.** Each unit covers a specific area of work. Some units are mandatory and some are optional.

- **Mandatory units** – these are units you *must* do. In your NVQ 1 Administration award there are **three** mandatory units. These are also called **core** units.
- **Optional units** – these are units you can choose to do. There are two option groups in NVQ 1 Administration:
    - optional group A, where you choose between paper-based filing or using a computer
    - optional group B, where you choose between helping customers or dealing with mail.

You must choose **one** unit from each optional group, i.e. **two** units altogether. Therefore to gain the complete award you will do **five** units in total.

Each unit is divided into two or three **elements**. Each element represents a different aspect of an area of work that you have to do.

Studying for an NVQ

You will study for an NVQ in two ways:

- you will learn about important areas of work so that you understand
  - what to do (and what not to do!)
  - why you should do it
  - how to do it properly and professionally.

You will do this by learning about all the topics included in the **knowledge and understanding** section of each unit (see page vii).

- you will practise carrying out the tasks you need to do so that you are good at them. The word you will often hear is **competent**. To gain your NVQ you have to prove you are competent at carrying out certain tasks and doing certain jobs. 'Competent' means you can do the job over and over again to the same high standard.

Proving you are competent

You will do this in the following ways.

- By showing your **assessor** how you work. You can do this by doing a job whilst your assessor is present. Any documents you produce when you are doing a task can be counted as **evidence** towards your NVQ – as long as you produced them yourself in a working situation.
- By proving to your assessor that you understand what you are doing and why you are doing it. This is sometimes obvious when you are doing a task, but at other times you may have to answer questions to demonstrate this (either verbally or in writing).

Storing evidence

You will collect a considerable amount of evidence for different units whilst you are doing your NVQ. Storing it safely is *very* important. In addition, because you are learning to be an Administrator, your assessor will also expect it to be neatly filed and properly organised – unit by unit!

Most NVQ candidates store their evidence in a **portfolio**. This is normally an A4 ring binder or lever arch file which contains documents relating to their job which they have created, prepared or used.

You will start your portfolio almost as soon as you start the scheme. Your portfolio becomes very valuable and must always be kept in a safe place. Losing it would be disastrous unless you have kept a copy of all your evidence.

Guidance on your NVQ – and the people involved

Your **tutor**, **trainer**, **adviser** or **supervisor** will be the person who helps you. It depends upon where you work and where you are taking your NVQ award. Regardless of the title, this is the person who will guide you on setting up your portfolio, help you to understand the scheme and what you need to do and show you how to provide the right kind of evidence.

As you complete each unit, an **assessor** will check all your evidence to make sure that it meets the requirements of the scheme. Your assessor may be your tutor or trainer or could be someone else. At certain intervals, an **internal verifier** will check particular units in certain portfolios. Don't be surprised if your assessors and your internal verifier want to talk to you about your evidence – they should do this so that they know who you are and how you have obtained your evidence.

An **external verifier**, sent by your awarding body, will also examine a number of portfolios as a final quality check. Your awarding body is the organisation which will issue your final certificate, such as OCR or Edexcel.

You will not know which units in your portfolio may be checked by a verifier. However, if your assessor has passed them, this usually means they are fine.

Check it out!

The first thing you need is a copy of the scheme. This lists all the units and elements. Obtain a copy now – if you have not already done so. Don't try to understand the whole scheme the moment you receive it. Instead look at unit 101 on team work which is the first mandatory unit covered in this book.

- The first page of the unit is a **summary** which identifies all the things you have to do.
- The next three pages explain the three **elements**. They state what you must always do and the evidence you must provide in each case. Specific additional evidence is also listed that you need to provide in certain circumstances.
- At the end of the unit the **knowledge and understanding** requirements are listed.

All the knowledge and understanding requirements are covered in this book. In addition, the evidence collection sections match the evidence listed in the scheme. By the time you have finished each unit you should feel confident that you could answer questions to prove your understanding and know how to provide the evidence required.

Starting out

Organising your portfolio – step one

The next step is to start your portfolio. You will need a set of dividers to separate each unit. You will also need tracking sheets or other documentation provided by your awarding body. Your tutor or assessor will give you these and tell you how to complete them.

Personal information – step two

It is always better if anyone assessing or verifying your portfolio knows who you are and what you are doing! You therefore need to start with:

- a title page, which states your name and the scheme title, i.e. NVQ Administration level 1
- information about yourself. If you are working, this should include:
  - your CV
  - your job description
  - your own version of your job description, which says in your own words what you do every day
  - a short description of your organisation, what it does and the people you work with
  - you can include an organisation chart if you want, but only do so if this would help people who read your portfolio to understand your own job better.

  If you are a full-time student, provide:
  - your CV
  - details of any work experience you undertake
  - details of any part-time job you have where you may be obtaining evidence towards your award (e.g. on working as a member of a team or dealing with customers)
  - details of any work placements you have in your own organisation, such as in a college office or training office.
- a list of all the people who are helping you to provide evidence, such as witness testimony (see below), and the names of tutors or advisers or supervisors who have added their signature to any evidence you have produced. List these clearly using the following headings:

  Name of person   *Job title*   *Sample signature*

Unit evidence – step three

Each unit will probably start with a tracking sheet. This is because you need to link your evidence to specific parts of the scheme. Your tutor or adviser will show you how to do this.

You may then be asked to write a brief **storyboard**. This is a short summary which says what you have done in relation to the unit or element. It helps to guide the assessor and verifiers. It is a good opportunity for explaining what you know and understand about the topic – and can save you time having to answer verbal questions. Again your tutor or adviser will tell you how to write a storyboard. If you are working, it is better if this is on letter-headed paper and signed by you *and* by your line manager at work. This confirms that what you are claiming really happens.

More about evidence

Evidence is proof you can do a task and understand it. However, you do *not* have to fill your portfolio full of paper to gain your NVQ award – there are other ways in which you can prove you can do something. However, as administrators often deal with paper, it is likely you will include some **documentary evidence**, as it is called, so we will deal with this first.

Documentary, or paper, evidence can be described as:

- **primary** – or **personal** evidence – which is very valuable
- **secondary** evidence – which is much less valuable.

Unfortunately, many candidates like to fill their portfolios with paper – regardless of its value! A few examples should help you.

Identifying primary evidence

The best evidence comes from **working documents** *you* have produced, or written on, or somehow made your own. They could include:

- a typed list of jobs you have been given, but on which you have made notes about what you are doing and ticked off each job when it has been done
- a copy of a photocopying request you received with a copy of the finished document you produced and a note from the person for whom you did the work, saying you did it according to instructions at the first attempt
- a diary or log you kept over a period of time which listed the jobs you did relating to a particular unit
- a typed document you prepared with the draft or original version attached, plus a note clearly showing the instructions you were given.

Never think that evidence is better if it is clean and pristine! A beautifully printed document may be the final result, but your evidence is much more valuable if you show all the scribbles and notes you made on drafts beforehand. This really proves that you had a personal involvement with the work.

Identifying secondary evidence

Secondary evidence is documents prepared by other people, which may have given you information. Examples include:

- formal health and safety policies you have been issued
- photocopies from books – such as this one
- photocopies of documents from files and office manuals.

None of these really counts for anything *on its own* and will not help you to achieve your award.

The only time you should use this type of evidence is if you can 'convert it' into primary evidence by doing something positive with it.

For instance, if you issued a brief safety sheet on operating a new photocopying machine *then* you could include a copy of the pages in the instruction booklet that you used as a basis of your safety sheet. However, you need to highlight what you decided to use and what you decided to leave out.

Other types of evidence

It is not practical to think that there will always be a piece of paper to prove you can do something. Sometimes this is not appropriate and there are much better ways of checking what you know and what you can do. **Activity evidence** can include the following.

- **Observation by your assessor**. Some people find this a bit unnerving – especially if it is a special occasion. It is better if your assessor can simply watch you working in a normal situation. You can then prove easily that you can put files away properly, photocopy, deliver mail and so on.

  Normally your assessor will then provide you with an observation report to go in your portfolio.

- **Witness testimony**. This is a document provided by a colleague of yours, or your supervisor or line manager, confirming that you regularly do a particular job well, or that you have provided help on a certain occasion. Witness testimony must be specific, however! You cannot ask your boss or tutor to write five lines to say you are good at everything and just get your award! Again, your tutor or adviser will give you advice.

  Witness testimony should be written on headed paper and signed by the person who wrote it – not you! The signature should be included on the list at the front of your portfolio. If you write a statement saying what you have done this must be countersigned to prove it is authentic (i.e. real and truthful). Normally, however, you will write your own version in your storyboard.

- **Oral questioning**. Your assessor may find out what you know and understand by talking to you and asking you questions. This should be more of a conversation than an oral 'test' and is done to check if you understand why you have done something – or to find out what you would do in a particular situation that hasn't occurred whilst you have been undertaking your award. You may be given a list of the questions you have been asked to put in your portfolio, together with a summary of your answers – or you can even include an audio tape on which your conversation has been recorded.

Final notes on evidence

There are certain other points you should know about evidence.

1 All your evidence must be **recent** and **sufficient**. This means that you cannot put in one piece of paper which is five years old to provide all your evidence for one unit!

2 Your evidence must be **relevant**, i.e. it must meet the requirements of the unit as specified in your NVQ scheme.

3 All your evidence must be **authentic**. This means the evidence must belong to you and must relate to *your* work.

4 You should not take confidential documents or sensitive information away from work without your supervisor's permission. Often such documents can be used once certain information has been blanked out – or your supervisor may agree to provide witness testimony instead

5 You can use evidence *in more than one unit* – if it clearly meets the requirements of both. This is called **cross-referencing**. It will save you extra work if you can identify opportunities where you can use evidence more than once. Again your tutor or adviser will give you help until you get used to this.

6 The best type of evidence is that which is **naturally occurring**. This means that you produce it as a natural part of your job. It is a good idea, whilst you are undertaking your NVQ award, to start a box file and put into it copies of documents you produce and evidence of work you have undertaken – so that you can use this to find appropriate evidence when you get to later units in the scheme.

The structure of this book

This book has been designed to help you in the following way.

- Each of the mandatory (core) units is covered in detail in the Core Units section, pages 1–121.
- Both optional group A units are covered, in slightly less detail. Remember you have to choose *one* of these two units.

- Both optional group B units are covered in the next section. Remember that again you have to choose *one* of these two units.

- The final section gives you information on applying for a job and advice on attending an interview. Many NVQ 1 Administration candidates later apply for full-time jobs or to be Modern Apprentices and these sections will help you to do this successfully.

- In addition, on the Heinemann website you can access information to help you improve your writing skills, improve your number skills and understand your rights and responsibilities at work (see page iii).

Special features

In each unit in this book there are special features to help you.

Key skills signpost

There are key skills signposts in each unit to help if you are taking your key skills award. Discuss with your tutor which signposts are useful for you – as you may not be taking all six key skills units.

The signposts indicate the most logical key skills unit(s) to link to that NVQ unit and suggest the tasks you can carry out to obtain most, if not all, of the evidence required for your key skills portfolio. In some cases the evidence links so well that you merely have to refine and extend your evidence a little to cover both the NVQ and the key skills unit. In other cases you will have to undertake additional work to obtain evidence.

You can, of course, use evidence from *any* NVQ unit to help to achieve some key skills units – such as Communications. Your tutor or trainer will give you further details.

The signposts have been written for candidates taking Key Skills units at level 1, but in every case the evidence can be extended relatively easily if you are studying a particular unit at level 2. Discuss the changes you would have to make with your tutor or trainer.

Check it out!

These sections give you the opportunity to find out information for yourself – often linked to the tasks and facilities you are currently using at work or at college.

Information update

Here you will find the latest information on a particular subject or area, linked to what is currently happening in business organisations.

Test your knowledge and understanding

These sections give you the opportunity to check how well you have understood information you have already covered. Sometimes these are in the form of a quiz or self-assessment.

Evidence collection

These are possibly the most important sections of all! Here you will find guidance, hints and tips on obtaining evidence to cover a particular section of a unit.

Again these sections *contribute* towards your evidence. On other occasions your competency may be assessed in other ways, such as by doing a task or questioning. Just collecting documents doesn't mean you have completed a unit! Again, your tutor, trainer or assessor will give you guidance on this.

SPECIAL NOTE

1   The knowledge and understanding sections in this book have been written to help you to test that you have a clear understanding of the information which you have just read – and to enable you to check any topics about which you are uncertain with your tutor or trainer. These sections may be used to contribute to your knowledge and understanding evidence, but the extent to which you need to provide additional evidence will be up to your assessor. Sometimes you will be able to prove that you understand something by the way you carry out a task, or by talking to your assessor about it. Therefore, do not automatically expect that you will have nothing else to do to prove you understand something after you have read through a unit and done these exercises!

2   Similarly, the evidence collection sections are intended to *contribute* towards your evidence and help you to identify opportunities for obtaining appropriate evidence *throughout* the unit. However, on many occasions your competency will be assessed in other ways, such as by specific performance or questioning. Therefore, simply collecting a number of relevant documents does not mean that you have necessarily completed a unit. Again you will be guided by your tutor, trainer or assessor on this.

Choosing your option units

Your NVQ scheme comprises:

- 3 compulsory units – which you must do.
- You have to choose one unit from the optional group A units. These units relate to selecting *either* paper-based filing *or* using a computer to enter and find data.
- You then need to select one unit from the optional group B units. You can choose between helping to maintain customer service *or* distributing and dispatching mail.

If you are at work, it is sensible to choose the options which link most closely to the job you do every day, so that you can obtain the evidence from your job as it 'naturally occurs'. It is sensible to talk to your supervisor at work before you make your final choice – especially if you are not sure which would be the best ones to do.

If you are not working yet, and will be obtaining evidence largely through placements in a training office or college office – or on work experience – then you should discuss with your tutor which options would be best.

Upwards and onwards!

You will probably find your NVQ award quite strange at first – just because it is so different. However, when you are familiar with it you won't find it hard, although hopefully you will find it a challenge. Anything which is too easy quickly becomes boring!

NVQs are good because they are practical. At work, no-one wants a 3-page essay on photocopiers – they want you to be able to use one to produce good quality documents when you are asked. They want to be able to depend upon you in a crisis to do excellent work, quickly, without panicking.

Your NVQ will help you to do this. Hopefully, when you have completed it you will feel a real sense of achievement. You will certainly be more valuable to any employer. You may even want to read the optional units you chose not to do for this award – to develop your skills in these other areas as well.

Your next step is then to move on to developing your skills, knowledge and abilities to a higher level.

Good luck!

Carol Carysforth-Neild
Mike Neild
August 2001

Contribute to effective team work

This unit is concerned with:

- how you work with other people as a member of a team
- how you organise your own work
- what you can do to continually improve yourself.

It is important because:

- at work, you normally work alongside other people
- these people will depend upon you to do a good job
- you can't do a good job if you are disorganised
- you won't get on with other people if you let them down or are uncooperative
- there are always new things to learn – no matter how much you know now
- moving forwards will give you a goal to work towards, which will help you to get on in life (and earn more money!).

There are three elements to this unit. Before you start these you need to understand why teams are used in business and why they are considered so valuable.

Your contribution to effective team work

You may not be friends with everyone at work but if you get on well with other people at work then doing your job is much more enjoyable. Getting on with your colleagues is often called having good **working relationships**.

Many people today work in **teams**. A team is a group of people who:

- have the same aim (e.g. to produce a complicated document, to finish a particular task by Friday)
- work together co-operatively to achieve that aim
- help and support each other – especially when things get tough.

A team can be very beneficial, because individuals all have different strengths and weaknesses. You may be good at IT, someone else in the team may not be, but may be better at working with numbers. A third person may be good at organising things. Between you, you have more strengths than any one single person.

Effective teams

An **effective team** is one where:

- the members have a mix of skills which *together* enable them to do a range of different tasks well
- the group is well organised
- the members put the achievements of the team *above* individual achievements
- they know each other's strengths and weaknesses
- in a crisis, everyone pulls together.

Contributing to an effective team isn't always easy. It means:

- putting the team first and yourself somewhere behind
- getting on with other people even if they annoy you at times
- remembering to thank people who have helped you
- not taking all the credit if you receive a compliment because of something achieved by the whole team
- sharing the blame when someone else in the team makes a mistake (and *never* saying it wasn't your fault)
- being loyal – on good days, bad days and ordinary days.

However, there are benefits. If you work as a member of a team, then you have people to talk to if you have a problem. You can also enjoy celebrating team successes and achievements with them, too!

I knew Robert would always want to do his own thing!

Teamwork should mean that everyone pulls together

The people who make up your team

You could belong to several teams, for example:

- Everyone in your organisation has to work towards a common purpose – the success of the organisation. If the people in marketing increase sales, everyone may share in a bonus.
- There may be ten people working in your office but you share a job with another person. You take turns to look after reception, answer the telephone, deliver and collect messages and mail and do the filing. In this case, you are a small team of two within a larger team.
- In another situation, you might work as an administrator in the office of a large CD/record store. Part of your job is to ring through to someone in the distribution warehouse to update orders, chase late deliveries and deal with urgent requests. It could be said that you and the person in the warehouse are a team.

At first sight, you may not use the word 'team' to describe these situations. However, if you look at the attributes of effective teams in the last section they all apply. Try it!

Test your knowledge and understanding

In teams of three or four, decide your *group* responses to each of the following questions.

1   For any team sport you follow, identify one team which is very effective and one which is not. For a moment, forget your normal loyalties and see if you can identify *three* reasons why there is this difference between the two teams you have chosen.

2   a   Your team has been given the task of deciding on the best place for a day out for all your group or class. You have 15 minutes to decide:
   i)   where to go, and
   ii)   the amount to charge people.
   Ask your tutor to time you.

   b   Work out how effective you were as a *team* when you did the activity above. This does *not* mean deciding which team had the best idea or was the quickest. It means finding out if everyone in the team contributed and had their say. If one or two members think they were ignored, or if one member took over, then this isn't teamwork – so score yourselves down!

   c   From your answers to **b**, what could you improve if you worked together again as a team?

Team responsibilities and their importance to the organisation

Many teams have targets and every team has the responsibility for doing certain tasks. Other people in the organisation will rely on the team to do these on time and to the right standard.

- **Targets** identify which jobs must be done and the date by which they must be completed.
- **Tasks** are the range of jobs they have to do.

Rubia's team, for instance, has to organise interview evenings at a college. Their target is to make sure all applicants receive a response within a week of making their application and are offered an interview within four weeks. This means:

- sending out acknowledgement letters promptly

- sending out letters to applicants giving the time and date of the interview
- noting down the applicants who say they cannot attend (so that new appointments will be made)
- preparing a list of people who will attend for members of staff
- making sure all the rooms are neat and tidy
- preparing the folders of information to give to interviewees
- greeting interviewees on arrival and directing them to the correct room.

Perhaps you attended college for an interview before you started a course. Think about what might happen if Rubia's team did not do their job properly.

- Applicants will receive a late acknowledgement letter – or no letter at all.
- Applicants may get interview letters too late to be able to attend on the date specified.
- Those who can't attend might never be given another date.
- The staff would have an incorrect list – or no list at all.
- The rooms would be a mess.
- The prospective students wouldn't receive the right information – or any information at all.
- They would have no one to help them on arrival.

In the end, they might decide to go to another college and Rubia's team could cause a severe problem if many students made this decision.

The same applies in any organisation. Whatever job you do, it is likely that the customer will be affected by any job you do badly – or don't do at all. So every team is doing a very important job. If it doesn't do the work properly and customers go elsewhere, then eventually the business would have to close down completely.

Maintaining good working relationships with other team members

This topic is dealt with in more detail later in this unit. For now, simply remember this. If you are a normal, average person then in every team you will find:

- people you naturally like and find easy to get on with
- people you wouldn't normally have much to do with, but with whom you can work quite well
- people you don't like and/or you find it difficult to get on with.

In your private life you can suit yourself who you see and who you are friendly with. At work you can't. You are paid to get on with everyone as best you can.

Test your knowledge and understanding

1   In the following situations, identify:

   a   who is part of each team

   b   whether this is an example of good or bad teamwork.

   i   Teresa works in the finance department and has run out of paper for the fax machine. The next delivery is due tomorrow. She asks Pitesh in marketing if she can borrow some. Pitesh refuses even though he has plenty.

   ii   The boss gets annoyed because the office is untidy. He tells everyone it is a tip and must be cleared up immediately. Everyone drops what they are doing and helps to tidy up – not just their own work but 'communal areas' such as around the photocopier and on the top of filing cabinets. All except Sam, who is nowhere to be seen.

   iii   Max passes his driving test – first time! The day after there is a congratulations card on his desk signed by the team leader, all the staff in the office (including Alex, who Max doesn't get on with) and a couple of people in other departments Max often works with.

2   Select one example of poor teamwork above and discuss what you would do, if you were the team leader, to try to improve the situation. Then suggest how the team members themselves could help.

   Discuss your ideas with your supervisor or tutor.

3   The following is a list of the top eleven irritants in an office, according to Internet company IntY.* However, in this case they have been muddled up! Decide, preferably as a group, in what order you would put these.

1	Computer breaking down
2	Rude colleagues
3	Too many interruptions or meetings
4	Lack of support
5	Having to share a desk
6	Awful tea and coffee
7	Colleagues eating at a nearby desk
8	Having too much work to do
9	Colleagues who smell or who have bad breath
10	Noisy colleagues
11	Missing an important deadline because something you needed didn't arrive in time

   *Research carried out by NOP

Element 101.1   Organise your own work

How well organised are you? Before you start this element, do the quiz below and find out how you score.

Check it out!

Answer each of the following questions *truthfully*. You don't have to tell anyone the result!

1   If you put something important away (like your passport), can you:
   a   find it again in two minutes
   b   find it after about half an hour
   c   never remember where on earth it went?

2   Are the clothes that you wore last night:
   a   either hung up again or in the washing basket
   b   flung over a chair
   c   still on the bedroom floor where they fell?

3   When you have been given assignments or homework which must be handed in to a deadline, do you:
   a   always hand them in promptly
   b   hand *most* of them in promptly (depending upon your other commitments)
   c   normally have to think of a good excuse, because you've forgotten to do them?

4   How quickly can you normally find your keys?
   a   Very quickly – they are either in your pocket or easily found in your bag.
   b   Relatively quickly, once you've turned out your pockets or your bag.
   c   Don't ask. You don't even know if you've lost them again . . .

5   When you have finished working anywhere, does your desk and the floor around you:
   a   look as clean and tidy as when you started
   b   look a bit of a mess
   c   need an army of cleaners to put things right?

6   The phone rings at home and you take a message for someone. Would this be:
   a   neat, easy to read and contain all the important facts
   b   a bit scruffy, but generally understandable
   c   the source of a major row afterwards because nothing you had written made much sense.

The importance of being organised

Being organised means:

- you can find what you put away
- you make realistic plans and then follow them
- you honour your commitments to people (i.e. you do what you say you will do)
- you are on time for everything – whether at college, work or meeting friends
- you keep things neat and tidy
- you write down things you must remember
- you normally meet your task deadlines, unless there is an unforeseen problem.

It's their own fault. They left it too late to find a decent tree.

Failing to plan ahead can cause problems

Your employer has to be able to trust you – and everyone else – to do all these things automatically. Otherwise the place would be chaotic and no business would be done at all.

The importance of organising your work

Organising your work means:

- knowing what you have to do
- doing jobs in the right order, i.e. doing urgent or important tasks *first*, even if you were given them last

- being methodical
- having the right tools and equipment close at hand and in good condition
- not putting off jobs you don't like doing
- doing the work properly *first time*
- completing work by the deadline or warning your boss in good time if you have a problem.

If you organise your work properly, you will be able to complete your jobs more easily and to a higher standard. You will gain a reputation for being both organised and efficient.

Understanding instructions

You will receive instructions to do work both verbally and in writing. Verbal instructions can be more tricky, especially if they are given quickly or when you are doing something else.

You will stand a better chance of getting it right if you:
- listen carefully
- concentrate on what is being said
- don't interrupt until the speaker has finished
- ask about anything you don't understand.

It is often tempting to pretend you understand instructions – even when you don't – in case the person thinks badly of you for querying them. Yet you are more likely to look silly if you do the job incorrectly – or do the wrong job! For that reason it is important to make sure you completely understand any instructions you are given.

Check instructions by:
- asking someone (politely) to slow down if they are speaking too fast
- asking someone to explain a word, expression or technical term you don't understand (if you are new to a job, you can't be expected to know everything yet)
- always repeating *back* a verbal instruction – to check you have understood it correctly
- asking a more experienced colleague to help you to decipher bad handwriting or a term in a written document you don't understand.

It is also important to remember what you are told!
- Always **write down** a verbal instruction or the right version of a word you couldn't read or understand.
- Always write down jobs you are given on a notepad – not on a scrap of paper which can easily get lost

- Put a 'star' next to urgent or important jobs – so they stand out.
- Always tick off jobs you have completed – then you can quickly check what is left to do.

Using time efficiently

If you ruin a sheet of paper you can use another one. If you run out of paperclips you can ask for some more. If you waste an hour of your day then that hour has gone forever. No-one can give it back to you. For that reason, time at work is very valuable.

If you waste time you will find yourself with jobs left over at the end of the day, when other people have cleared their desk. So, what type of things happen to make you 'waste' time? These can include:

- talking to people about things unconnected to work, such as where you went last night
- not concentrating, so you have to do a job again
- having a messy desk or losing things, so you can't find what you need to start a job
- not understanding or liking a job, so you play around with other things instead of starting it
- spending too much time doing what you like to do, rather than what you should be doing.

You will use time more efficiently if you:
- have a tidy desk
- know where to find everything you need
- keep the items you use regularly in working order, e.g. the stapler full of staples
- do the most urgent, important or hardest jobs when you are at your best

- stick to a job until it is done (then reward yourself with a short break)
- think ahead – so you take all the post to the mailroom at once or do batches of photocopying, for instance, and don't have to keep running backwards and forwards
- do 'little jobs' when you have a few minutes spare (such as filing a few papers whilst you are waiting for the printer to finish printing a long document)
- check your list of jobs regularly throughout the day and *always* about an hour before the end of the day to see if there is anything which must be done before you leave.

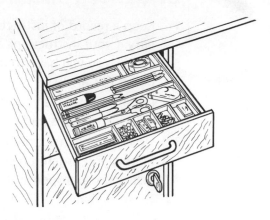

How would your desk drawer compare?

The things you need – and keeping them organised

The exact items you need depend upon your job role. Large, expensive equipment should be situated nearby but will be shared between several people. Smaller items should be available for everyone.

The 'big' stuff includes:
- a desk to call your own, with drawers in which to keep items you use regularly
- a swivel chair of your own, which supports your back properly
- a computer (if you produce documents) and printer
- a telephone or the shared use of one
- filing cabinets for office documents
- stationery cupboards for office supplies
- a fax machine
- a photocopier.

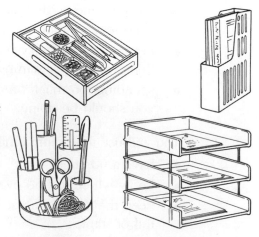

Desk accessories can help you to be organised

The 'little' stuff you need includes all kinds of stationery, from pencils to paperclips. Many routine items used in an office will be stored centrally. Packets of photocopying paper will be near the photocopier, with the rest in the stationery cupboard. File folders, printer paper and so on will also be kept in a stationery cupboard. Although you may have a small stationery supply of your own, it isn't normal to keep half a box of envelopes on your desk unless there is a specific reason for this!

Test your knowledge and understanding

1 Shahid's boss, Greg, is in a hurry as he is going out for the day. Just before he leaves he rushes into the office to see Karen, Shahid's team leader. Karen isn't there so Greg quickly speaks to Shahid.

'The staff noticeboard is a disgrace. Half the stuff is way out of date and should have been thrown away weeks ago. We've some important visitors tomorrow, so make sure it's sorted, will you? Oh, and my printer's playing up again and needs seeing to. I'll be back at 5 and it would be helpful I could print the odd piece of paper by then. Finally, can you make sure someone puts the Gibson file on my desk, I need it for the report I'm writing.'

   a How many jobs has Greg given to Shahid?
   b Luckily Shahid scribbled them down. But do you think Shahid should have checked the instructions? What made him hesitate, do you think?
   c Shahid considers going out to the noticeboard and tidying it up himself. Do you think this is a good idea or not? Give a reason for your answer.
   d Shahid is not sure whether to contact the printer supplier or an internal department. What do you think he should do?
   e What, exactly, do you think he should say about the printer fault when he does find out who to contact?
   f Shahid goes to the file and picks up the first file he sees with the name Gibson and puts this on his boss's desk. He is pleased he has managed to do this properly. What is your opinion?

2 Marianne has the following jobs to do today. In which order do you think she should do them and why?
   a file the copies of some documents she prepared yesterday
   b make a telephone call to a customer to change an appointment as the person she wants to see is away until Monday
   c photocopy some documents for a meeting next week
   d order some more photocopying paper – there's hardly any left
   e type a 3-page document which is needed for tomorrow morning.

Ordering stationery

When you need to order stationery you need to know:

- the system to follow in your organisation
- how to ask for what you need.

In many organisations, you must complete a form to request stationery. This may be called a **stationery requisition**. If stationery is only delivered once or twice a week, then you will have to plan ahead to allow for this. However, in most places you can obtain small items, such as pencils and pens, much quicker as a small quantity of 'buffer stock' will be kept in the office.

When you are completing a stationery requisition, you can't simply write down 'lots of envelopes' or 'some packs of paper'. You have to be specific and it helps if you know the sizes and types of items you need. The table opposite may help you.

Check it out!

1   Look through some stationery catalogues and identify all the items listed in the table opposite – and see how much they cost.

2   Practise folding A4 paper so it fits into a DL envelope properly. Now try folding it so the address would show in a window envelope. Ask your tutor or supervisor for guidance if you are having problems with this.

C4 envelope	**DL envelope**	**C5 envelope**	**DL window envelope**
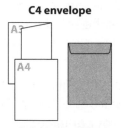		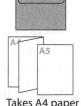	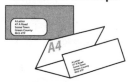
Takes A4 paper flat or A3 folded once	Takes A4 paper folded twice	Takes A4 paper folded once or A5 flat	Takes A4 paper folded twice according to guidelines so address shows **clearly** in window

Envelope sizes

Item	Information
Paper	Sizes – A4 (most popular). A5 (half of A4), A3 (double A4). A1 is the largest. Quantities – a pack of paper contains one ream (500 sheets). Colours – various but standard is white for general office use. Types – lined (for writing) supplied loose or in A4 pads. Unlined for printing, fax machines, photocopying. Various qualities and weights of paper, standard is 80 gsm weight but recommended best paper is given in each machine handbook. Bond paper is another term for good quality plain white paper.
Envelopes	Sizes – C4 takes A4 paper flat or A3 folded once, C5 is half this size, C6 is smaller still. DL is used for letters – takes A4 paper folded twice (see illustration on page 12). Quantities – often sold in multiples of 100. Colours – white (for most correspondence) and brown. Types – fastenings vary: can be gummed, self-seal or peel and seal. Wallet style – envelope opens on longer side; pocket style – opens on shorter side. Window envelopes popular as address on document shows through transparent 'window' and saves typing. Different weights – the heaviest are more prestigious but more expensive. Other types include heavy duty envelopes, cardboard backed envelopes (for photographs), airmail (very light weight) and padded Jiffy bags to protect fragile items. Labels are also available for printing computer listings of names and addresses.
Printed stationery	Types: letter headed paper is printed with organisation's details; compliment slips are smaller versions for inserting with general items sent by mail; fax cover sheets may be used or fax pads printed with name of organisation.
Folders	Sizes – foolscap and A4. Foolscap are slightly larger. Quantities – depends on type. Filing folders sold in 100s, more expensive versions sold individually or in 10s. Colours – various. Cheapest are brown. Types – filing folders (for storing papers in filing cabinets), document wallets have a flap to store or carry papers safely, project and presentation folders are more expensive and usually have transparent front cover.

Stationery sizes

Keeping your working area clean and tidy

Your working area isn't just your desktop. It includes all the areas for which you are responsible. So, for instance, if you do photocopying or greet visitors at the reception desk, it shouldn't be absolutely obvious you've been there because of the mess you've left behind!

If you are ever tempted to work in a muddle, remember there are several dangers.

- You are unlikely to find what you need quickly.
- You can throw away the wrong thing by mistake.
- You'll spend as much time looking for things as doing your job.
- If someone opens a window or door, you are in danger of seeing half your papers float onto the floor.
- You will feel under more pressure (because you are making your job more difficult).
- You'll probably annoy everyone else!

Organising your desk

Some people think that the only document on your desk should be the one you are working on. This is extreme, but you should really aim towards this. Useful tips include the following.

- Keep papers you are not currently using in trays or folders out of the way.
- Have your telephone within reach, so you pick up the receiver with your non-writing hand.
- Have a pen and notebook within reach at your writing side.
- Keep your desk tidy at the back of your desk – so you can't knock things over easily.
- Put small items of stationery you use regularly in your top drawer.
- Store larger or heavier items lower down.
- Keep spare paper in its packet or in a folder, to stop it getting crumpled.
- Have a proper system of working – so you get out what you need, use it and put it away again.

Finally, be aware of 'danger signals.' If you find you've papers on your desk, the top of two filing cabinets and on the floor as well, then **stop**. Have a clear up before you do anything else.

Organising other areas

If you share a working area with other people then having a proper system is even more important – whether you are photocopying or

making the coffee! It obviously helps if there is plenty of worki
such as a table on which to put items and ample storage areas
and files – or even cups and coffee!

Again your system should be:

- get out *only* what you need
- set it out neatly (don't spread it all over the place)
- use it
- put it all away again.

see next page.

Check it out!

1   Chris has started a new job. On the first day she is told to list what she
    needs from the stationery cupboard. Chris does this but receives her
    list back from her supervisor with various comments – see next page.
    From what you know about stationery requirements, can you rewrite
    her list properly?

2   Chris is right-handed and the
    desk she has been given to
    work on is illustrated below,
    together with her computer.

    Chris's desk

    a   Identify those items from
        the list which you think
        should go on her desktop
        and those which should
        be stored in desk drawers.

    b   Decide the best
        arrangement of items on
        the top of the desk.

3   During her first week at work,
    Chris hears staff talking about
    the following items of
    equipment. Find out what each one does and write a brief description.

    a   guillotine   f   shredder
    b   laminator   g   binder
    c   trimmer   h   long arm stapler
    d   zip drive   i   heavy duty stapler
    e   antiglare filter   j   scanner

Check your answers and ideas with your tutor or supervisor.

Chris's list

3 ring binders and dividers – *have you any preference on colour?*
Inkjet cartridge for printer – *colour or black and white?*
2 blue pens
2 black pens
pack of plain paper – *what size/colour? Do you mean a ream?*
letter headed paper – *is 30 sheets OK?*
compliment slips
Post-it notes
pack of lined paper – *A4?*
notebook
liquid paper
highlighter pen – *any particular colour?*
eraser
ruler
pencil sharpener
filing folders – *I presume you want brown A4? How many?*
document wallets – *how many? Do you want assorted colours?*
10 plastic pockets – *do you want the type punched with holes or the type open on two sides?*
pen cup (for pens and pencils)
letter tray (four – stacked)
desk tidy for post-it notes, paper clips, staples etc
mouse mat
diary
calculator
envelopes – different sizes – *do you want just white ones or brown, too? Please specify sizes. Do you want window envelopes too?*
scissors
stapler
staples
staple remover
hole punch
floppy disks – *how many?*
floppy disk storage box

Information update

According to an American study, personalising your workspace with pictures, photos or plants makes you feel better and helps you to work harder. This is because you take more 'ownership' over the area.

However, a word of warning! Some companies actively discouraged this as they thought it looked unprofessional.

Minimising waste

Many organisations aim to be environmentally friendly. They buy recycled paper and envelopes, recycle printer cartridges and waste paper etc. This, however, is pointless if all the wastepaper bins are overflowing with wasted paper at the end of every day!

Areas of your job where you need to take precautions to minimise waste include:

- **stationery**
  - Store it properly so it is kept in excellent condition.
  - Don't order more than you need.
  - Use it wisely (such as turning old paper into scrap pads and re-using envelopes you have received to send internal documents).
  - Don't use plastic wallets to store routine papers.
  - Reuse file folders by turning them 'inside out' and writing the new name on the other side of the tab.

- **document creation**
  - Always think before you start to write, so it doesn't take three attempts to write a brief message.
  - Check *all* typed documents very, very carefully on screen (use *both* your spell checker and proofread it word by word yourself) so the first print-out is usable.
  - If you are printing a long internal document, use the 'draft' setting on your printer to save ink or toner.
  - Don't take colour print-outs unless you have been asked to do so.
  - Back up your work on a clearly labelled floppy disk. Don't use a new disk for every document!

- **photocopying**
  - Check the original is in good condition.
  - Always do a 'test copy' first.
  - Never do more than you need (or a few extra for luck!).

- **communication**
  - If you are finding information on the Internet, check you know which sites to use and don't take more print-outs than are necessary.
  - If you have to 'dial up' the Internet, learn how to download information so you can print out 'off-line'.
  - Don't use the office telephone for personal calls, except in an emergency – and you should still ask permission first.
  - Make notes before you make a business call – so you don't forget something and have to ring again.

Check it out!

How much waste do you create at the moment when you are typing a document or using stationery? As a check, count how many sheets of paper you throw away each day – then try to reduce that number!

Evidence collection

Explain how you keep the items you need for your work organised and available. You can do this by:

- identifying the main items you use
- saying where you keep or store these
- explaining how you make sure your working area is as clean and tidy as possible.

For *three* jobs you routinely undertake, say what you do to try to keep waste to a minimum. Ask your team leader or tutor to confirm this.

Asking for help and support

Everyone needs help and support from time to time – and many people actually like providing advice or assistance. So don't be worried about asking for help when you need it. The important points to note are *when* and *how* to ask for it – and *who* to ask!

When to ask for help

- When you don't know how to do something.
- When you don't understand something.
- When you can't finish a job you agreed to do by the deadline – either because it's too hard or you have too many other things to do.
- When you have a problem you can't cope with on your own. This could be a personal difficulty, a problem with another team member or a problem with a customer, for instance.

How to ask for help

- Be polite. Saying 'please' costs nothing but can make all the difference!
- Be precise, e.g. 'Please can you show me how to rename this document on my computer?'
- Don't blame the equipment or anyone else, e.g. 'This package is stupid. It's impossible to do this.'
- Listen carefully and concentrate when you receive an explanation. It's impolite to look bored, to look away, be doing something else or to keep interrupting!
- Write down instructions that are long or complicated – so you have notes to refer to next time.
- If you are having problems completing a job on time, give your team leader plenty of warning. Explain why you are having a problem and be prepared to suggest how much help you think you will need.

- If you are having personal problems, or problems dealing with a colleague or customer, ask to talk to your team leader in private. You can expect the discussion to be kept confidential.
- Say thank you (and mean it!) if someone helps you in any way.

Who to ask

It is sensible to think about the best person who can help you.

- Ask your team leader or supervisor for help if the matter:
  - relates to work scheduling and allocation (i.e. who does what and when)
  - affects other members of the team
  - relates to your customers
  - involves you being away from work.
- Ask the best 'expert' (in your office or in another department) for help on specialist matters, e.g.:
  - a computer problem
  - a photocopier jam or break-down
  - a health and safety issue (see Unit 102)
  - a problem relating to your pay or tax.
- Ask a team member for help if the problem relates to work you do as a team, e.g.:
  - if a file is missing
  - if you receive a message you cannot understand
  - if you need a name and address or fax number and don't know where to find it
  - if you receive a complaint and don't know what to do
  - if you need help for a few minutes to enable you to finish an urgent job
  - if you need 'cover' at reception because you are having to leave the office for a few minutes. Don't just disappear!

Providing help and support to other people

Just as you need help and support, so do other people. Helping members of your team is dealt with on page 23. However, you may also be asked for help *by* other people, e.g.:

- staff in other departments in your organisation
- your customers
- other external suppliers and contacts, such as your suppliers or repair people.

Obviously you are expected to be cooperative and helpful, particularly if people just want routine information or to leave a message for someone.

However, this does not mean you should agree to every request. Seek help if you are asked:

- to do work for another department (this would normally need the agreement of your team leader)
- for information which is sensitive or confidential (such as someone's personal details).

In such cases, simply say you will have to refer their request to your boss or a senior colleague – and do so.

Meeting task requirements

When you are given a job to do, your work is judged by whether:

- you have followed the instructions you have been given
- you have used your common sense to sort out simple problems
- the final result meets the needs of the person who gave you the job
- the job is done on time.

If you suddenly encounter a serious problem with a job or make a mistake, you may worry that making a mess of it – or producing it late – will ruin everything. It may help to realise that *everyone* has these types of problems now and again – and no one is perfect. It's how you react in these situations that is important – not the fact that they occur.

If things go wrong	
Do	**Don't**
<ul><li>put matters right if you can, even if this takes time out of your break or lunch hour</li><li>if this is impossible, let your team leader know about the problem promptly</li><li>be positive – make suggestions how it can be solved</li><li>apologise if you have done something silly or are in the wrong (e.g. you hadn't checked your work)</li><li>learn from the experience.</li></ul>	<ul><li>sulk or go into a rage</li><li>pretend the problem doesn't exist</li><li>bluff your way out of it</li><li>keep telling everyone that things are fine.</li></ul>

Test your knowledge and understanding

Explain exactly what you would do in each of the following situations:

a   Your team leader has asked you to do some urgent photocopying – to be finished by 3.30 pm. At 3.15 the machine breaks down.

b   You have just printed an important document your boss is waiting for when you notice three typing errors on the first page.

c   You are asked to take a customer file to your team leader, who is in a meeting in another building some distance away. It is pouring with rain. As you arrive at the door of the room, you realise you have the wrong file in your hand.

d   You have collated and stapled some reports for a meeting which is being held at 4 pm. At the last minute, you realise you have forgotten to attach the front and back covers.

e   Your boss has asked you to find some information for him on mail services on the Internet. You haven't a clue where to start and he has gone out for the day.

Evidence collection

Explain at least three occasions when you have asked other people for help. Say why you needed help, who you asked and what happened next.

Give examples of when you have provided work on time and the actions you took to make sure it met the needs of the person who asked for it. Ask at least two people for whom you do work to confirm that you do this by providing you with witness testimony (see page x).

Support the work of your team

In this section you will learn more about working in a team and the type of behaviour which will help your team – and that which will not. However, occasionally you may have problems with some of your colleagues and how to deal with these is covered on page 28. Finally, you can see how good you are at communicating with other people – and find out how important communications are to the working of a team.

Key skills signpost

There are close links between this element and the Key Skills unit **Working with others**. If you are doing this unit at level 1, then you can link most of your evidence for this element towards your key skills unit.

WO1.1   You must be able to show that you understand the aims or objectives of your team and help to identify how these could be achieved and ways in which you could help. You also need to show you clearly understand your own responsibilities and working relationships.

WO1.2   You need to prove you can work with other people to do tasks for which you are responsible and work safely and accurately, following the working methods you have been shown. You must also show you can ask for help and offer support to other people when appropriate.

WO1.3   You must prove you can identify what has gone well when working with other people and identify any difficulties you encountered. Then show you tried to do something to overcome these problems and suggest how you could improve the way you work with other people in the future.

For **evidence** you could use:
- confirmation or records from someone who has been present when you have had discussions with other people about teamwork and objectives
- a list of your objectives, responsibilities and working arrangements with confirmation that you understand these
- your own notes or records of how you have carried out tasks in a team
- your own notes of how and when people helped you and you helped them
- confirmations by other people of the way you have worked or how you have helped them
- photographs of any team event you have been involved in with contributions by other team members as to your role and responsibilities
- your own statement on your own progress as a team member, with comments from your team leader or other team members
- records of your answers to questions about any difficulties and how you coped with these
- your own ideas and suggestions on how to improve the way you work with other people in the future.

Helping team members

You will always be expected to help your team members when you can. In addition, your team can expect (or hope) that you will remain relatively calm and cheerful in a crisis. They will also expect you to pull your weight. All teams are very wary of people who don't!

Did anyone see where Bill went?

When to help – and when to refuse

No matter how naturally helpful you are, it is important to realise your limitations in providing help and support.

Help other team members when:

- you can spare the time
- you are willing to 'make' time (e.g. by staying late to help or giving up part of your lunch-hour)
- you know how to do the job (or are willing to learn)
- the job is an 'official' one which your team is supposed to do
- a team member is worried or upset and you can give practical help and assistance.

Test your knowledge and understanding

Shazia is known for being kind and always willing to help. Sometimes this means she is 'put upon' which worries her. Today she has received the following requests. (Read the text at the top of page 24 before you do this.)

a Which do you think she should help with – and which should she refuse? Give a reason for your answers.

b What do you think she should say to each person?

   1 A team member asks her to lend a hand for 5 minutes to help unload a delivery of photocopying paper.

   2 Her friend, who works in another office, rings and asks if Shazia could bring a box of floppy disks with her at lunchtime when they meet. Apparently, the other office has run out of them at present.

   3 Her team leader asks her to do an urgent job before she goes for lunch at 12.

   4 A colleague asks if she will stop what she is doing and look after reception for half an hour. The time now is 11.30 and Shazia still hasn't finished the job her team leader wants doing.

Apologise for not being able to help if:

- you are so busy yourself you'd miss your own deadlines if you stopped
- you have a commitment which means you can't stay late to help out
- you have no idea what to do and showing you would take too long
- the person is involved in something which your team leader or manager wouldn't approve of
- you would be giving away confidential information.

However, there is nothing to stop you suggesting that your team leader may be able to give useful advice.

Evidence collection

Give examples of occasions when you have given support and help to *either*:

- your line manager or team leader
- other people in your team.

If you can, identify occasions when you have been asked for help but felt you could not provide this. Say why you could not and what you said to the person who asked you.

Essential information

In every job you will deal with information. Some of this will be essential and the rest will be routine. How do you decide which is which – and what you should do when you receive important or essential information?

Identifying essential information

Essential information is that which is important – and should be passed on to the correct person *immediately*. One method of identifying essential information is to consider the consequences of *not* doing anything.

You can consider information essential if:

- it is received from a senior manager or an important customer
- it relates to a current sale
- it relates to the delivery of urgent supplies or an urgent repair
- it relates to a job your team is doing at the moment
- it will affect someone's future plans

- it involves a serious complaint
- it relates to a family crisis or problem for another team member
- the person who provides the information mentions the words 'important' or 'urgent'.

Although you may be very hesitant to interrupt people to give them routine information by mistake, if you are in any doubt remember that people would normally rather you did this, than *didn't* pass on an important message. Always go for 'safe' rather than 'sorry'!

Test your knowledge and understanding

You work in a team of five. You have a team leader, Marie, and four colleagues – Kelly, Sinead, Karl and Saeed.

You receive the following items of information today. Identify:

a which items are essential and which items are not

b what you should do with each item of essential information

c what the consequences would be of *not* doing anything with it.

1 Sinead has a young son. His school telephones to say he is ill and should be taken home. Sinead is currently in a meeting with Marie.

2 The canteen phones to say their boiler has broken so there will only be cold drinks at lunchtime.

3 You get a call from a customer to say that the items they ordered from Karl haven't arrived today as promised. Karl is on a training course today.

4 A salesman from your stationery supplier arrives and leaves you their new catalogue and price list.

5 Computer services ring to say there is a fault with the network and all computers will be 'down' from 3.30 pm that afternoon until the following morning.

6 You receive a call from the finance department to say the meeting Marie was attending tomorrow morning has been postponed until Friday.

7 Marie rings to tell you she only needs 30 copies of a report she asked Saeed to copy and not 50 as she originally thought.

Communicating essential information

It will be helpful to remember the following points.

- Check you have noted down all the facts correctly.
- Pass it on promptly.
- Pass it on verbally if the person is nearby. Otherwise write out the information clearly.

- Make sure you actually *hand* the information to the person who must receive it. *Don't* leave it on a cluttered (or empty!) desk.
- If you need to interrupt someone – or interrupt a meeting – apologise (for the interruption) and simply hand them the written message.
- If the person isn't available, tell a senior colleague or your team leader.

Evidence collection

Identify at least four occasions when you have received important information. Explain:

- what the information was
- what you did to make sure your team members received it as soon as possible.

Working relationships and behaviour

The first step in developing good working relationships with other people is to realise they are human! They have preferences, they have faults, they have funny ways of doing things. Just like you!

Check it out

Study the table opposite that shows the type of behaviour which helps to develop and maintain good working relationships in a team – and that which does not.

Try a simple test. Think about yourself and think about your friends. Then ask yourself the following.

1   Do you find it easier to spot 'faults' in your friends' behaviour than your own – or the other way round?

2   Why do you think other people's faults are more often obvious than your own?

3   If you are more apt to think of *yourself* as being at fault all the time, what could you do to improve your own view of yourself?

The bottom line is, no one is perfect and no one is always at fault!

Working relationships in teams

Helpful behaviour:

- listening to – and trying to understand – other people's points of view
- being loyal (e.g. not gossiping or talking about people behind their back)
- being helpful and supportive
- allowing for other people's 'ways of doing things' or 'idiosyncracies'
- counting to 'ten' if you feel you are losing your patience
- not saying (or writing) anything you may regret later
- helping out when you can
- explaining why you can't give help, if it is impossible or difficult – not just saying 'no'
- not interrupting people when they are busy, unless it is essential
- being polite and courteous at all times and remembering the simple words, such as 'please' and 'thank you'
- being tactful and not making hurtful remarks because you respect other people's feelings
- being cheerful and nice to be around – *but* also being sensitive to other people and their situations – so you don't tell someone how happy you are when you can see they are obviously miserable
- not expecting other people to 'bail you out' because you haven't done your own job properly.

Unhelpful behaviour:

- being childish, e.g. sulking, being moody or throwing a tantrum
- always wanting your own way
- being jealous or resentful of other people and their successes
- blaming other people (or life in general!) for problems
- doing sloppy work that other people have to redo
- finding reasons not to help which are obviously excuses
- being economical with the truth if you are asked a direct question (in other words, telling lies!)
- being impatient or irritable the second you are under pressure
- complaining or moaning about the job, about how much you have to do or about other people
- sighing – whenever you are asked to do something
- being negative and always seeing the problems but never the solutions
- being tactless, rude, insensitive and ignoring how other people feel
- being disloyal, gossiping, telling tales unnecessarily.

Problems with working relationships

No matter how hard you try, it is inevitable that at times you will have differences of opinion with other team members. If the person is senior or older than you, then you may have to back down gracefully no matter what you think. If the person is your own age then you could end up having an argument. Even senior colleagues may give you problems if you feel they are often being unfair to you.

What should you do in this situation?

Solving the problem yourself

As a first step, see if minor adjustments in your own behaviour would help, for example:

- If the disagreement is about something specific, listen carefully to the other person's views. Then decide why you are so opposed to them. Does it really matter? Could you live with their idea? If this is impossible, could you reach a compromise?

- If you feel the other person is being unfair, try to state how you feel – without being too emotional. For instance, 'Every time I suggest something you always turn it down. I know I can't be right all the time but this makes me feel really useless. Could you spend a few minutes telling me what I'm doing wrong?'

Test your knowledge and understanding

Discuss – as a group and with your tutor:

a what has 'gone wrong' in each of the following situations

b what you could do to *try* to put things right.

1 You and Lisa are responsible for taking the mail to the post each night. You quickly realise that every time it's raining Lisa finds another urgent job to do. You accuse her of this and she goes mad and accuses you of trying to get her into trouble. Neither of you is speaking to the other at the moment.

2 A huge box of stationery has been delivered and 'dumped' outside the door to your office. It's in everyone's way. You have asked a team member to help you to move it but he says he's too busy. You say he isn't – he's just being idle. It needs moving urgently but both of you are sitting down, glaring at each other at the moment.

3 You think a senior member of staff is picking on you. Every time you produce a document she finds several errors in it. This morning she criticised a message you had taken and said she didn't understand it. You retorted that this was hardly surprising, given she's so dim. She has now reported your attitude to the team leader.

4 A new team member arrived on a day when you were working in a complete mess. Your desk was cluttered with paper and you had lost three files. He has now got it into his head that you are a comic act and regularly makes jokes about you to everyone else. You are not only fed up with these but find them hurtful and are upset that people are laughing about you behind your back.

Reporting problems to your line manager

No matter how much you may not like admitting defeat, there are some occasions when you *must* report problems to your **line manager**. Your line manager may be your supervisor, team leader or other person. However, the term refers to the person immediately superior to you at work.

Problems you should report include:

- continuing difficulties with an older or more senior member of staff
- problems which cause you embarrassment or discomfort
- problems you have tried to resolve yourself but cannot
- any occasions on which you are bullied or threatened
- any occasions on which someone seriously upsets you.

You should ask to see your line manager in private. Try to keep calm and not be too emotional – although this can be difficult. If you think the problem is really serious, and are nervous about talking to your line manager, you could ask an older colleague to accompany you to the meeting. If, for any reason, you do not think you can approach your line manager, then find another senior colleague who you trust to talk to.

You will help your manager if:

- you start by giving a clear description of the problem
- you give specific examples – rather than making wild accusations
- you state any actions you have taken to try to solve the problem
- you make it clear how this situation is making you feel.

Your line manager will take this seriously. He or she may make useful suggestions as to how you could change the way you are handling the situation. Listen carefully. Ask for time to consider these rather than simply find reasons why you shouldn't do any of them! You can also expect your line manager to want to talk to the other person as the next step. Do cooperate with this process – if you stop your line manager from doing or saying anything then it may be almost impossible to solve the problem.

Finally, you will find that most organisations work hard to solve any problems as quickly as possible. You may not get all your own way if there is a dispute between you and someone else, but a good manager will try to find a compromise which you both can accept. If, however, you ever work for an organisation (or manager) which does not take steps to help you, then either talk to the Human Resources manager or start looking around for other opportunities. Life is too short to be made miserable in any job – especially when there are so many other opportunities available.

Information update

All organisations have grievance procedures for solving problems officially which cannot be solved in any other way.

There are laws to protect people at work from bullying, harassment and discrimination.

- Bullying is when someone makes threats to you or makes your life a misery in some other way – such as by taunting or mocking you or showing you up in front of other people.
- Harassment is behaviour which you find embarrassing – such as lewd or suggestive remarks, abusive or racist remarks or intimate questions about your personal life. Both sexual and racial harassment are illegal and should be reported immediately.
- Discrimination is when someone treats you differently just because of your gender or race or because you have a disability of some kind. Today, everyone at work must be treated the same and given the same opportunities.

It is for this reason that serious complaints by staff are always taken seriously.

Test your knowledge and understanding

Shaun is a new team member who started last month. This week you are horrified that you have overheard him:

- deliberately telling a customer a product is cheaper than it really is
- saying your team leader is 'an idiot'
- making about six personal phone calls each day
- bragging about coming back from lunch late without anyone saying anything.

Tonight he calmly pocketed 6 pens and 2 boxes of floppy disks and winked at you as he left.

You are worried that if you tell your team leader everyone will think you are a tell-tale but don't know what to do.

Discuss your options as a group and with your tutor.

Communicating clearly

No team will ever work effectively if its members don't communicate with each other. Unless you tell people what is happening and keep them informed, they will not do their jobs effectively – and neither will you.

However, it is one thing to communicate and quite another to communicate accurately, clearly and promptly regardless of whether you are passing on the information in person, over the telephone or in writing. To be an accurate and reliable communicator you need a number of skills.

Will you all shut up –
I can't hear a word she's saying.

Face-to-face communication

Face-to-face communication includes any occasions on which you talk to one person, or a group of people, direct. Everyone at work has face-to-face encounters every day and most people have no difficulty with casual or informal conversations. The situation can be more nerve-wracking if the occasion is more formal, such as an interview for a job or talking to a group of people, such as in a team meeting when you may be asked to make suggestions. However, if you have developed good verbal communication skills, you are likely to have fewer problems. Ideally you need:

- a clear speaking voice
- to speak at the right pace (not in a mad rush, for instance!)
- a good vocabulary – so you choose the right words to use
- to think about what you are going to say before you say it
- a certain amount of tact and discretion
- the right tone of voice
- appropriate body language.

Let's look at these in more detail.

Today most people find accents and dialects interesting – no one tries to speak like a BBC announcer any more! However, if you have a *very* pronounced accent, or use slang a lot, then you may need to slow down a little and think about what you say if you want everyone to understand you easily.

If you are nervous or excited, it is tempting to speak very quickly. Again this can create problems. If you feel like this, take a few deep breaths before you start to speak and try to speak at a steady pace.

When you communicate with someone, you need to be able to say what you mean. Otherwise you can cause misunderstandings. So use the correct words to describe something properly. If you are worried about the meaning of a word, either look it up in a dictionary or ask a colleague for help. However, no matter how good your vocabulary, if you don't stop to think first, you may say something you didn't mean – or it may simply 'come out all wrong.' So think first – especially on important occasions.

Even if you choose the correct words, you will annoy or upset people if you are tactless or thoughtless. Sometimes you may have to pass on information to someone else and it may be better to rephrase a remark you have heard (or ignore it altogether).

Your body language should match what you are saying

Finally, all your efforts will be in vain if your tone of voice is wrong or your body language doesn't 'match' what you are saying. Body language relates to the facial expressions you use, the gestures you make and the way you stand or sit. An obvious example is saying you are sorry whilst you are smirking or raising your eyes upwards. No one would be very convinced!

Communicating on the telephone

Many people are nervous when they first make or receive business telephone calls – even if they are never off their mobile phone normally! They are worried they won't understand what is being said or won't know how to answer. This is not difficult if you remember a few basics.

The important facts you need to know are shown on page 34. This table tells you what you *should* do – and what you *shouldn't* do – when you are receiving or making a business telephone call.

Check it out!

Check through the table overleaf now. Identify those business telephone skills you think you already possess – and those you think you need to practise and develop.

Then, with a fellow student or a colleague who will help you, practise making and receiving telephone calls. Even though you will be working face-to-face rather than using a telephone, you can role play this and it is more effective if you try not to look at each other! If you are short of ideas then try the following:

1 One of you is buying some office stationery from different suppliers and has to ring through several orders. You will need to prepare for this by making a list of items and quantities. If you want to make it more realistic, both use a catalogue to obtain and check product codes and prices.

2 Your boss has said you can replace your chair with one which will swivel and provide good back support as you do a lot of computer work. Ring through to several suppliers and ask what types are available and how much they cost. The other person should have information available on prices and types.

Business telephone skills	
DO	**DON'T**
Receiving a call • answer promptly • identify yourself – say the name of the firm, your department or your name, depending upon the normal greeting in your organisation • have a pen/pencil and notebook to hand • speak clearly and hold the mouthpiece properly so you are speaking into it • find out who the person wants to speak to. If this person is available then transfer the call (either by passing over the receiver or by transferring the call on your phone system) • if the person isn't available, offer to take a message – and write it out promptly	• try to rush the call • use slang, e.g. 'You what?', 'OK', 'Hang on'. • cover the mouthpiece and shout to someone else – the caller will hear everything you say • worry if you cannot understand an important word e.g. the caller's name. Ask the caller to repeat or spell it out. You can use the phonetic alphabet the police use (**A**lpha, **B**ravo, **C**harlie) but any sensible word will do which works! Such as: 'I'm sorry, did you say Hewell? Is that H-E-W-E-L-L? No? Could you spell it for me please? Thanks. That's W for William, H for Harry, E-W-E-L-L. Whewell. • just scribble a quick note on a scrap of paper
Making a call • check you know the number to dial and the person to ask for • prepare for the call by writing down everything you need to say • introduce yourself clearly. State your name and the name of the organisation, e.g. 'This is Anna Shaw from Secure Software Systems'. Then ask for the person you want • as you mention each point, tick it off on your list • if the person has been very helpful you can conclude the call by saying 'Thank you. Goodbye.' • if the person you want is not available you will probably be asked whether you want to leave a message or ring back later. It is sensible to check when the person you need is expected to be available if you agree to ring later.	• panic if you are asked which department the person works in. If it is a large organisation, and the person you want has a common name, e.g. Smith or Patel, there may be several people who work there with the same name • gabble your name, so the person on the other end cannot understand you. Be prepared to spell your name if it is unusual • expect the other person to be able to guess what you want. State your reason for calling clearly • wait for the other person to conclude the call. This might happen but technically, because you made the call you should be the person to bring it to an end.

Taking a telephone message

There are *five* skills involved in taking a message.

1 **Listening** to what is being said to you. This means concentrating and not interrupting or doing something else at the same time.

2 **Understanding** what is being said. This means you must check anything you are not sure about by asking questions, e.g.:
   - ask for the caller's name and firm (or name and address)
   - ask for their telephone number (and read this back to check it)
   - ask why the caller is ringing and listen carefully to the reply. Bear in mind some people may not wish to give you this information because it may be personal or confidential.

3 **Identifying** the **key facts** in the message. You are not supposed to write down everything that was said, just the main points. These usually relate to:
   - **who** is calling
   - **the number** they are calling from
   - **when** they called
   - **what** they rang about
   - **dates** and **times** they mentioned
   - **how** they want the person they are calling to respond
   - **when** they need the response (e.g. any deadline).

   Always double check by:
   - writing down any numbers, times, days and dates – and checking them
   - repeating back any other important parts of the message
   - finding out if the message is urgent
   - finding out if your team member should ring the caller or if the caller would prefer to call back later.

4 **Writing** a proper message from your notes.

   Many organisations have pre-printed message pads for staff to use. These are useful because the headings remind you what to ask. With most pads there is also an automatic copy made, which is useful for reference.

   As you become more experienced you will be able to write directly onto the pad. However, to start you may be better writing on a scrap pad and only putting your final message on the form. This is because:
   - the information you write down may not be in a sensible order
   - some of your writing may be scribbles which another person wouldn't be able to read
   - you may need to check the spelling of some words
   - you need to use the right *tone* for the recipient. For instance, if you are writing a message for your boss, you shouldn't put 'you must ring Mrs Evans immediately'. This sounds like you are giving your boss an order! Instead it is far more tactful to write 'please can you ring Mrs Evans as soon as possible.'

5 **Passing** on the message. You have not done your job properly until the person who needs the message has received it. If it is urgent, you must find them or tell someone else.

Never put a telephone message in the normal mail tray. In this case, the recipient may not see it until tomorrow morning – or even later if they are away from the office for some reason.

Check it out!

1 Find out if your employer or college uses telephone message forms and then try to obtain some examples on which you can practise taking messages.

2 Kelly works for Zenith Communications. Look at the notes Kelly made below and how she used these to prepare the finished message. Identify:

   a the order in which she rearranged her notes
   b the words she changed – and why
   c the extra information she included which isn't shown in her notes
   d the tone she used.

   Discuss the reason for these changes with your tutor or supervisor.

Kelly's notes

> *Mr Brown (Jack) –*
> *Whitestones Garage Car*
> *service*
>
> *Sarah's car. Could do it*
> *Monday 16th or Thurs same*
> *week*
>
> *Clio*
>
> *Must have it by 8.30.*
>
> *Drop off night before = post*
> *keys thru letterbox*
>
> *Ring back 01298-398393*
> *Ask for Jack*

Zenith Communications

To: *Sarah Spencer*

From: *Jack Brown*
      Whitestone's Garage

Tel No: *01298 398 393*

☑ Please Ring Back   ☐ Will Ring Back

☐ Returned Your Call   ☐ URGENT

Message: *They can service your Clio on either Monday, 16th March or Thursday, 19th March. They need it at the garage by 8.30 am but if you prefer you can take it the night before and post the keys through their letterbox. Please ring Jack and tell him which date you prefer.*

Date: *9/3*   Time: *10.05*   Taken By: *Kelly*

Written communications

Almost from your first day at work you will be expected to write short notes and messages which:

- other people can read and understand easily
- contain all the relevant information
- have no obvious errors or 'howlers'.

Composing communications for other people to read isn't easy, but some useful hints and tips include:

- typing the message if your handwriting is poor
- using a spell-checker on a computer
- making sure you include your own name so that people know who the message is from
- always putting the date on a message, so people know when you wrote it
- writing short sentences
- never using words you don't understand
- if you are quoting a day or a date in a message, always write *both* as a double check, e.g. Monday, 25 June
- using names when you are talking about two people of the same sex – if you keep using 'he' or 'him' it's easy to get confused
- carefully reading it through yourself, to check it makes sense
- asking someone else to check it, if you're still worried
- improving your written communication skills if you feel these let you down.

Information update

Today most organisations use e-mail. You may use it yourself – as anyone can have a hotmail account and send e-mails to their friends from college or cyber-café computers.

If you work for such a company, you will have your own e-mail address and will be expected to send short messages and information by this method. However, this means your communication skills are instantly on show for everyone to see.

Test your knowledge and understanding

1   You also work for Zenith Communications. Your team leader, Andrew, is having a bad day. He is looking for your colleague, Perveen, who is on her break. Convert what he says to you into an appropriate message you could give Perveen, verbally, when she comes back.

'Where's Perveen? Having a break? Good heavens, does that girl never stop eating? Why's she never around when I want her? Anyway, give her this back will you. Ask her to make the corrections I've noted and add page numbers and then it's OK. I need 20 copies before 4.30. It might be better if she uses the copier on the top floor – the one down here's on the blink at the moment.'

2   Before you can do very much Andrew returns, this time waving a piece of paper in one hand. He is in a fury. 'Who on earth wrote this?' he says 'What do you all think I am, psychic? Find out what's going on will you!' With that, he hands you the paper and stamps out.

The paper Andrew was waving about is shown here.

a   Why do you think it annoyed him so much?

b   What can you suggest to solve the problem – both now and in the future?

3   You receive the following call on the answering machine when you return from lunch.

a   Convert it into a proper written telephone message for Andrew and write this on a copy of the form on page 237.

'Hi, it's – er – 12.30 and I was hoping to speak to Andrew. It's Sean MacIntyre here from Jepson's Couriers. He wanted to know if we could get a parcel of his over to France by Thursday. I thought it was impossible but I've now found I've a driver free. We'd need to pick it up by 9.30 on Wednesday morning, though. Ask him to let me know, will you. Preferably before 3 o'clock this afternoon. My direct line is 06718-298718. Cheers.'

b   Andrew isn't in his office when you take the message to him. What would you do?

4   Andrew prefers all requests for time off to be in writing. You want to know if he would agree to giving you next Friday off work as a personal day's holiday. You have been offered the chance to visit the Motor Show in Birmingham with a friend and would very much like to go.
Draft a note, asking for his permission, and then ask your supervisor or tutor for an opinion on whether you could have worded it any better.

Element 101.3

Contribute to your own learning and development

This element is concerned with you – and your future plans. It helps you to identify how you can identify areas to develop and what sort of activities will help you.

Key skills signpost

This element has close links to the Key Skills Unit **Improving your own learning and performance**. If you are doing this unit at level 1, then you can link most of your evidence for this element towards your key skills unit.

LP1.1   Discuss your short-term targets with your line manager or team leader and agree how these will be met. Make sure your targets on your learning plan show what you want to achieve and include deadlines and a review date. Identify how to get the support your need and when your progress will be reviewed.

LP1.2   Use two different methods to improve your performance:
- study a straightforward subject
- learn through a straightforward practical activity.

Show how you have worked through your learning plan to complete tasks on time and identify the support and help you received from other people. Explain the different ways of learning you have used and how and when you have changed these when it has been necessary.

LP1.3   Review your progress and achievements by identifying:

- what you have learned and how; what has gone well and what has not (and the reasons)
- identify targets you have met and what you have achieved
- decide what to do next to improve your performance.

For **evidence** you could use:

- two copies of your completed learning plans
- a diary or log to show how you followed your plan
- your own notes on the help you have received
- records from people who have helped you or seen your work
- examples of your achievements, such as work you have done or skills you have learned. This should cover two subjects and two practical activities
- notes on your learning plan to show targets you have met
- your own review on what you have learned and how, what went well and what did not and what you would like to do next.

Developing yourself in a team

As a team member, you have two types of people to deal with:

- your team leader or line manager
- other team members.

If you are sensible, you will deal with them slightly differently. No matter how informal or friendly your team leader or line manager may be, this person is *still* your boss! You would not, therefore, normally talk to this person in quite the same way you would to team members – especially those of your own age. You will be expected to:

- comply with direct requests
- be polite and give respect for position and seniority
- if you have a good reason for holding a different point of view, say so carefully and tactfully and not in front of other people!

A good rule of thumb is to treat your bosses as they treat *their* bosses! With other team members you will be more informal – although probably rather less so with older or more experienced members of staff.

As you become more experienced in your job, you will hopefully want to develop your skills and abilities. One of the most useful ways of establishing what areas you can develop is to obtain **feedback** on the work you do at the moment.

The importance of feedback

Feedback is comments – either formal or informal – that other people make to you about your work. This may be complimentary or not. It depends upon how fast you work, your accuracy, your attitude and how well you contribute to the work of the team as a whole. The most important thing is that feedback is *fair*. If you know you aren't very good at something, and someone points this out, then you should be prepared to consider the remark fair, even if you didn't like it!

Feedback from your line manager or team leader

You should know what your line manager or team leader thinks about your work. In some organisations, there are regular sessions when your work is reviewed and the good points – and areas for development – are discussed. In others there are not. However, if you regularly get work back to redo, this should make you stop and think. Equally, if your manager is always praising you, then you can be fairly sure he or she is generally satisfied with what you do. But this is still a bit of a guessing game, which is why review sessions are so valuable.

As part of this scheme you have to ask your line manager or team leader for feedback. Before you receive this, it is sensible to prepare for the discussion yourself:

- what do you *know* you are good at?
- what do you *think* you are good at – but would like another opinion?
- what do you *think* you should improve?
- what do you *know* you should improve?

In each case, try to think of examples to support your view.

Feedback from other people in your team

This is likely to be more informal. However, in some organisations staff are appointed a mentor to help them. This is another team member who they can turn to for advice, help and to discuss any problems. A mentor should be a more experienced member of staff who can advise you and help you to avoid any pitfalls. A mentor is an ideal person to ask for feedback on your progress.

If you haven't a mentor, then you should ask a more experienced team member for their views – rather than your best friend. A friend won't

Feedback can be very useful

want to say anything negative and may be embarrassed at having such a discussion with you.

Coping with feedback

Positive feedback is wonderful. Everyone likes being told how good they are! However, negative feedback, or criticism, is harder to cope with. It is very easy to get upset, to think you are useless, to forget all your good points – or even to lose your temper in defence. Negative feedback doesn't mean you are a bad person. It means there are one or two areas you could improve. Very few people are so wonderful there's nothing they couldn't do better. The main point is that successful people *learn* from their mistakes, so that they don't repeat them. So try to think about your skills and abilities as separate from you as a person.

You can 'test' the fairness of negative feedback by asking for specific examples. If someone says 'you need to improve your proof-reading skills' – and you think there's nothing wrong with them – ask for evidence. If they remind you that last week you had to retype seven documents then it is hard to argue any more. If they can't remember when you last made a mistake, then this is rather different.

Whatever you do, if you receive a criticism, therefore:

- don't take it as a personal insult
- ask for examples
- don't blame other people, the weather, the way you felt or the mood you were in that day
- be prepared to take responsibility for what you can and can't do
- ask for suggestions about improving your weaknesses and obtaining other skills
- boost your confidence afterwards by reminding yourself about things you used to struggle with and are now good at doing.

Evidence collection

You have to prove to your assessor that you have asked *both* of the following types of people for feedback:

- your line manager or team leader
- other people in your team.

Keep a record of your feedback sessions. In particular, note down areas of your work which you were told were up to standard and areas other people – or your line manager – thought you could improve.

Explain how you coped if you received feedback which included any criticism – so that you could stay positive and still focus on your own future improvement.

Learning plans

At the end of a feedback session you should feel good and focused on the future. You should know what you are doing well and what you could do better. You may have also had the opportunity to say what new skills or abilities you would like to learn in the future.

Once your goals have been agreed then it is sensible to write down a summary of these, so you won't forget them. This is usually done on a **learning plan**.

Your learning plan should state:

- what you have agreed to learn or improve
- the time-scale over which you intend to do this
- the methods and activities you can use
- the date on which your plan will be reviewed and progress (or lack of it!) noted
- the name of the person you will review it with.

There are many different types of forms used as a learning plan, and you may be issued with a special one by your employer or your college.

Check it out!

An example of a learning plan which Jackie Marsh completed, in agreement with her line manager, is shown on page 44. Work through this with your tutor or supervisor. If you wish, you can take a copy of the blank learning plan on page 238 to use for your first plan.

LEARNING PLAN

Name   Jackie Marsh   Date plan started   5 September 2002

Employer's name or College   J C Evans & Co Ltd

Name of reviewer   Sally Kent   Review date   31 January 2003

Development aim	Target date	Activity	Outcome (✓ when achieved)
Complete NVQ 1 Administration	June 2003	College course	
Improve telephone message taking	November 2002	Work alongside Carla Cox (mentor) for three weeks	
Learn to rectify paper jams on photocopier	December 2002	Training by Declan O'Sullivan – team member	
Improve spelling and punctuation	June 2003	Take Key Skills level 1 Communications at College	
Improve word processing skills	June 2003	Study for RSA Word Processing stage 1 at College	
Learn mail handling procedures	December 2002	Work in mailroom for 3 weeks during November.	

To be completed before the next review by employee or student

Identify any areas still outstanding. If these should have been completed by review date, give reasons for non-achievement.

Signed ....   Date ....

An example of a learning plan

Learning styles

Jackie Marsh agreed to undertake various different activities as part of her development plan. These show you there are various methods of learning new skills and abilities.

- Sometimes you can watch someone at work. This is sometimes called 'work shadowing'.
- Sometimes you can be trained at work. This is valuable if you need to learn a special type of equipment or a software package.
- Other times you may attend college to learn and achieve a specific qualification.
- Another way is to 'have a go' when mistakes won't matter, such as practising creating 'example' documents on a word processing package.

There is no overall 'best' way; it depends upon what you need to learn and how you learn *best*. Another way of identifying this is to find out your own **learning style** because everyone learns in slightly different ways.

Thinkers and do-ers

- Some people are very practical. They would rather do something than talk about it.
- Other people prefer the theory. They may like to think or talk about computers all day, but do not like using one very much!

The rash and the wary

- Some people like new things. They enjoy a challenge and get bored quickly. They like life – and work – to be very varied.
- Other people are more careful. They like to know everything before they make a decision or do something new.

I said flap **both** wings at the same time!

Words and pictures

- Some people learn best by looking at pictures and diagrams. They normally represent ideas graphically too.
- Other people prefer words. They would rather make a list than draw a diagram.

You may have been able to look at these options and make a choice each time as to the best way you learn. But you often have to adapt your style according to the situation in which you find yourself.

Test your knowledge and understanding

For each of the following situations, identify:

a which would most naturally suit your learning style

b how you can adapt your learning style for the others.

  1 Your supervisor is giving you detailed information about the procedures to follow if you receive a complaint from a customer.

  2 The team member who logs orders on the computer database is going on holiday. You've been asked to learn how to do this as quickly as possible.

  3 Your team recently organised an open day. There were several problems and your team leader wants to discuss why these occurred and how they can be avoided next time.

  4 Although you have heard a lot about the Internet you have never used it properly. When you first start, it isn't really like you expected and you have to change your ideas quite a bit.

Reviewing your learning plan

You should have noticed that at the bottom of the learning plan on page 44 there was a section for Jackie to complete before she has her next review. Reviews are important. If they did not happen there is a temptation to put the learning plan in a drawer and forget it. However, whether the review is pleasant or something dreadful depends upon:

- how much you have achieved
- whether you did even better than expected in certain areas
- whether there is a good reason for any non-achievements.

'Good reasons' in your view, of course, may not be the same as good reasons identified by your tutor or team leader! To minimise any differences (and avoid any arguments!) you can safely assume that:

- unavoidable external events and personal problems are 'good' reasons
- procrastination (look up this word!) is not!

The danger is that you put off doing something until the last minute and then panic whilst you try to catch up. If you are prone to doing this then your *planning* skills are poor – and should be added to your learning plan to be improved! You will not learn anything properly if you are simply trying to do it to put a tick in a box. Neither will you enjoy it. If this is happening you need to have a long, hard think about what you *really* want to achieve and what you would enjoy doing.

Test your knowledge and understanding

Which of the following reasons do you think Jackie's team leader would think was a good reason for non-completion and which would he not? Give a reason for your answers and then say what you think Jackie's team leader will suggest in each case.

1 Jackie didn't improve her message taking skills because:
  a Carla was off sick
  b Jackie herself was off sick
  c she was too busy with her other work and never got round to it.

2 She didn't learn how to rectify paper jams because:
  a a new photocopier was installed so the session was delayed until Declan learned it properly
  b there haven't been any paper jams for months
  c Declan's wife had a baby and he was on paternity leave in December when he should have been showing Jackie how to do this.

3 She didn't learn mail handling because:
  a she went one day but didn't like it
  b the mailroom supervisor asked her to wait until the New Year
  c she didn't think it would be of any use.

4 She didn't complete her Key Skills in Communications because:
  a she'd got behind with her NVQ and spent the time doing that
  b she doesn't like Key Skills
  c her mother was very ill and she couldn't attend college .

Evidence collection

Keep copies of your learning plans. For each one make sure you show:
- what you agreed to do to improve your work
- what activities you agreed to undertake to support your plan
- what you achieved and did not
- when it was reviewed
- what was agreed at the review.

It will help your assessor if you either write or describe verbally what happened in your reviews and what you now think you are doing well and could improve in the future.

Unit 102 Ensure your own actions reduce risks to health and safety

This unit is concerned with how to:

- identify the hazards and evaluate the risks in your workplace
- reduce risks to health and safety in your workplace.

It is **important** because:

- accidents can happen in any workplace – not just on building sites and in factories
- health and safety risks affect you and your colleagues
- you have a legal responsibility to be responsible for your own health and safety and to cooperate with your employer about health and safety matters.

There are two elements to this unit. Before you start these you need to understand about your legal responsibilities, to be able to recognise common hazards and to understand the difference between hazards and risks.

Key skills signpost

If you are taking your Key Skills award in Application of Number at level 1 then you can extend your knowledge of health and safety as you work through this unit and use this as evidence for your Key Skills portfolio.

Two of the tables in this chapter and the work you will have done with them as part of your knowledge and understanding self-tests will also contribute.

N1.1

You need your work in relation to the tables on pages 58 and 82, which state:

- the amounts by which organisations were fined for breaching health and safety laws during 1998/9
- the injuries to employees in offices by types of accident during 1998/9.

N1.2

1   Complete the task on page 59, which asks you to undertake various calculations to the table on fines to organisations and to draw a pie chart.

2   Complete the task on page 81, which asks you to undertake various calculations with the table on injuries to office employees and create a bar chart and line graph.

3   Measure the office in which you work or an office area at your college and calculate the area. Take measurements of major pieces of furniture and equipment. Work out what fraction of the area of the room is taken up by furniture and equipment.

Draw a scale plan on a diagram of the room and assess it for safety. Could any items be moved or changed around to improve the working environment? Give reasons for your decision.

4   Calculate *both* the volume and, if possible, the weight of at least four large rectangular objects (such as a large box of paper, a filing cabinet and two other objects). Decide which items are too heavy for you to lift alone and which you can manage safely. Summarise your findings.

If possible, compare your results with those of other people in your group. If certain members can safely manage heavier weights than others, see if you can find out why. (They may have undergone special weight training, for instance.)

5   Many employees grumble if it is too hot or cold in an office, yet the definition under health and safety is 'reasonable'. This normally means not less than 61°F, but there is no fixed upper limit.

   a   Today most temperatures are given in Centigrade. Find out how to convert Fahrenheit to Centigrade and convert 61 degrees Fahrenheit to its Centigrade equivalent.

   b   Take the temperature in your office or classroom over a period of a month. Draw a chart to represent your findings and calculate the *average* daily temperature in Centigrade.

   c   Decide whether you consider the temperature is 'reasonable' in terms of health and safety and give a reason for your answer.

d Suggest what temperatures you think would be too hot or cold to work in. Do this by experiment, rather than guesswork! For instance, take the temperature inside your fridge and outside the house on a cold night, find out how hot it is next to a radiator or fan heater. Compare the temperature of rooms at work or college that face north and face south and see if there is a difference. Then suggest what you would do if the heating broke at work in winter or if you were asked to work next to a window on a sweltering day.

N1.3

Present your work by preparing a summary of all the tasks and calculations you have undertaken and state what you learned from these.

List the checks you made to make sure all your answers made sense.

Your own actions in reducing risks to health and safety

A recent survey of 12 administrators in an office had the following surprising result. Nine thought that health and safety was relevant to their job but three did not. Health and safety is relevant to *everyone*. You don't have to do dangerous work to be hurt. Many people who operate computers, for instance, risk injury to their neck, shoulders, back and hands if they don't sit properly.

Therefore, if you are sensible, you will take health and safety issues seriously because you could be hurt just as easily as anyone else.

Your legal duties

It is important to realise that you and your employer also have a **legal responsibility** in this area. This is because, in 1974, a major law relating to health and safety was introduced, called **The Health and Safety at Work Act**. For ease, this is often referred to as HASWA.

This Act says that all **employees** have:

- a duty to take reasonable care for their own health and safety, for instance by not playing dangerous practical jokes
- a duty to other people who may be affected by their actions (such as colleagues or visitors)
- a duty to their employer (or anyone else acting on his or her behalf) to cooperate over health and safety issues, for instance by obeying safety rules.

In addition, all **employers** must provide:

- safe entry and exit routes in and out of the workplace
- a safe working environment
- well-maintained, safe equipment
- safe storage and transport of articles and substances (such as heavy or dangerous items)
- protective clothing where required
- information and training on safety and supervision for new or inexperienced workers.

Check it out

1   Find a copy of the health and safety poster in your workplace or college and *read* it. Look for a large heading **Health and safety law** with the initials HSE at the right-hand side. Below this are the words 'What you should know.'

2   HSE stands for Health and Safety Executive. This is the government body responsible for health and safety. Linked to this body is the HSC – the Health and Safety Commission. You can find out a lot more about the work of the HSE if you have access to the Internet. Their web address is www.hse.gov.uk.

3   Over one million workers a year currently suffer a work-related injury and have an average of two weeks off work. The Chairman of the HSC claims this costs Britain £18 billion a year.

Statistics show that:

- more men than women have accidents *regardless* of their occupation
- workers and trainees in their first year of a new job have more than twice as many accidents as those who have been employed over a year.

As a group, can you suggest any reasons for these two findings?

4   Identify under which sections of the Health and Safety at Work Act each of the following would be an offence.

   a   You refuse to wear a hard hat as you cross a building area because you think you look silly in it.

   b   You wedge open a fire door in a corridor because you are tired of pushing it open.

   c   Your friend insists on using the lift to leave the building when the fire alarm sounds.

   d   When the photocopier breaks down, you are told to 'sort it out' even though you have no idea what to do.

In organisations where there is a recognised trade union, safety representatives must be appointed to investigate accidents or employee concerns.

In addition, every organisation with more than five employees must provide a copy of its health and safety policy and make this available to all staff. The main terms of the Act must also be displayed in the workplace. You will see this at work or college or in any training establishment.

Information update

The dangers of amateurs trying to do jobs they are not trained to do was highlighted recently when television programmes such as Ground Force and Changing Rooms were held responsible for a 27% increase in accidents in the home and garden. According to the Royal Society for the Prevention of Accidents, both programmes disregard basic safety rules and encourage people to work too quickly. They also show skilled professionals doing work that amateurs think they can copy.

Dangerous activities seen on television have included:

a man using equipment without tying back his long hair drilling into brick and sanding floors without wearing safety goggles
lifting heavy weights such as bricks and boulders
laying a cable across a lawn rather than on the perimeter (where it is far less likely to be cut by accident).

Seventy people died doing DIY in the home last year – many by electrocution. This was often caused by trying to rewire or repair an appliance without disconnecting it and turning off the power first. Electricity and electrical appliances should always be left to the experts – both at home and at work.

Legislation covering your job role

There are very many regulations relating to health and safety. In this unit, the regulations are divided into two categories. Both are *equally* important.

- Category A affects all employees or relate to many office duties.
- Category B is likely to affect you but probably less often.

Category A – Workplace (Health, Safety and Welfare) Regulations

In 1992, the Workplace (Health, Safety and Welfare) Regulations were introduced. These are of interest to all employees because they relate to the health, safety and welfare of everyone, no matter where they work. The requirements for each of the main sections are as follows.

- **Work environment** – effective ventilation; reasonable temperature; adequate and emergency lighting; enough space; suitable workstations; protection from bad weather for those who work outside.
- **Safety** – separate traffic routes for pedestrians and vehicles; safe floors, windows, skylights, doors, gates and escalators; guard rails on stairs and landings
- **Facilities** – adequate toilets, washing facilities, sufficient seating for staff, fresh water, rest areas and provision for pregnant women/ nursing mothers; provision for non-smokers in rest areas; facilities for people who eat at work or need to change clothing at work.
- **Housekeeping** – proper maintenance and cleanliness of all facilities.

Category A – Display Screen Equipment Regulations

This is a very important set of regulations for all employees who use a computer, although you will see the term VDU (visual display unit) used, rather than the term 'computer'. You will also read the term **workstation**. This is your complete working environment – your desk and working surface, your chair and all the parts that comprise your computer equipment, e.g. your screen, processing unit, mouse, keyboard and printer.

Key
1. Adjustable seat
2. Firm back support
3. Adjustable seat height
4. Swivel action
5. Foot rest if needed
6. Space for freedom of movement, no obstacles under desk
7. Forearms approximately horizontal
8. Minimal wrist movement
9. Screen set at height and angle to allow comfortable head position
10. Space in front of keyboard to rest hands/wrists

NB Armrests are optional, but not essential.

Correct seating and posture are important

The Regulations relate both to the use of VDUs and the design of workstations.

All **employers** must do the following.

- Make sure that all workstations, the working environment, furniture and computer software of computer users meet the minimum requirements of the Regulations.
  - **Display screens** must have a stable image, the characters must be of an adequate size, the brightness and contrast must be easily adjustable, the screen unit must tilt and swivel easily and there must be no reflective glare.
  - **Keyboards** must be tiltable and separate from the screen with enough space at the front to provide a 'rest space' for your hands. They must have a matt surface, be easy to use and the symbols on the keys must be clear to see.
  - **Work surfaces** must be large enough for the work being done and have a low reflective finish. The equipment must be capable of being arranged to suit the needs of the user.
  - **Work chairs** must be stable and allow easy movement and a comfortable position. The seat height must be adjustable. The back of the seat must be tiltable so that it provides good back support. Foot rests must be provided on request.
  - **The working environment** should provide satisfactory lighting but keep glare to a minimum. Windows should have blinds or workstations be placed to avoid reflections. Noise and heat levels should be comfortable. Radiation levels must be negligible and humidity controlled so that the air is neither sticky nor too dry.
  - **Software and systems** must be suitable for the work being done, be user-friendly and appropriate to the level of knowledge of the user.
- Make sure that all VDU users have regular breaks or changes in activity. It is illegal for them to work continuously at a computer all day.
- Arrange for an eye examination, on request, for those who use a VDU for more than one hour a day, and provide special spectacles if the test shows these are needed.
- Provide all users with adequate health and safety training about their equipment.

Category A – The Provision and Use of Work Equipment Regulations (PUWER)

All offices contain equipment – photocopiers being the most obvious. These Regulations relate to the position of such equipment and how it is used and maintained.

- Large items must be positioned safely, where they will not be knocked or banged, and in accordance with manufacturer's instructions. For instance, a large photocopier needs to be on a level surface, with a good air flow all around it and there must be room for the operator to work safely.

- Equipment must only be moved by someone who has been trained or instructed how to do this.

- Staff must receive proper training on how to use equipment and be specially trained if they will undertake routine maintenance operations – such as rectifying a paper jam.

- The wiring of all electrical equipment must be checked regularly by a qualified person and there should be sufficient sockets so that no wires are trailing and adaptors are not required.

- Equipment checks and maintenance must take place regularly. This is especially important for complex equipment and machinery which is used frequently.

Category A – The Manual Handling Operations Regulations

These Regulations are concerned with lifting and moving items, especially heavy ones. You may not think office staff do this regularly, but you will change your mind if you ever have to help to move stationery deliveries. Paper is very heavy!

- All organisations must provide trolleys or wheeled 'sack' trucks to lift and move heavy items.

- Electrical equipment must be disconnected before it is moved.

- Staff must never try to lift a load which is too heavy and should be trained how to lift properly – by bending the knees first, not the back, so the strain is taken by the legs. Your legs can cope with this, your back cannot!

Category A – Fire Precautions Regulations

Most business premises must have a fire certificate giving a plan of the building and showing the position of fire-resistant doors, fire extinguishers and break-glass alarms. There must be a proper fire alarm system and specially protected means of escape. This means it must be well marked and kept clear.

It is very, very important that all employees know what to do if there is a fire. For this reason, you will have received instruction on this on your first day at college or during your induction in a new firm. Even on a training course, one of the first things the organisers do is to explain the fire drill. Visitors to many organisations find the fire drill printed on the back of their visitor's badge or card.

Added to this, there are always fire notices around a building. These state what to do if the alarm sounds and where the assembly point is.

Check it out!

1   Write down the action you must take if the fire alarm sounds whilst you are at work or college.

2   If the fire alarm sounds, you must not use a lift.
    a   Why do you think this is so?
    b   Find out, in your college or workplace, what you must do to help a wheelchair user who is with you on an upper floor when the alarm sounds.

3   All visitors have to hand back their badges when they leave a building. This procedure is closely linked to fire precautions. Can you suggest what the link is?

4   Your friend is late for his part-time job when the fire alarm sounds, so he decides not to bother going to the assembly point.
    a   What could be the consequences of his decision?
    b   Under which part of the Health and Safety at Work Act would he be committing an offence?

Category B

These Regulations are summarised in the table on the next page.

Employers' Liability (Compulsory Insurance) Regulations

All employers must take out insurance against accidents and ill-health to their employees. This means that if any employees are injured at work, they can claim compensation. Their claim would be met by the insurance company. This Regulation prevents any organisation from claiming it could not afford to pay compensation.

Reporting of Injuries, Diseases and Dangerous Occurrences Regulations (RIDDOR)

Organisations must notify the HSE of any serious or fatal injuries and keep records of certain specific injuries, dangerous occurrences and diseases.

Control of Substances Hazardous to Health (COSHH)

Hazardous substances must be stored in a special environment and users provided with protective clothing and instructions on the use and storage of such substances.

Electricity at Work Regulations

These relate to the design, construction, use and maintenance of electrical systems.

Noise at Work Regulations

Employers must check noise hazards and reduce these where possible and provide ear protectors to employees where necessary.

Management of Health and Safety at Work Regulations

Employers must carry out risk assessments, eliminate unnecessary risks, control significant risks and provide information on risks to all employees.

Health and Safety (Safety Signs and Signals) Regulations

All organisations must display safety signs to identify risks and hazards. There must also be written instructions on how to use all fire-fighting equipment. All safety signs must be to a specified design and in the correct colour.

Personal Protective Equipment at Work Regulations

Protective clothing and equipment must be provided when risks cannot be eliminated. This must be free of charge, fit properly and be maintained in good condition.

Health and Safety (First Aid) Regulations

There must be sufficient first aiders. The number depends upon the level of risk. A low risk workplace (e.g. most offices) should have one for each 50 employees.

Category B Regulations

Enforcing the law

There are three different bodies which enforce these laws.

- The HSE has its own inspectors. It also gives advice and guidance to employers and companies on complying with the law. An inspector can visit any industrial premises to investigate an accident or complaint or to carry out an inspection – without advance warning.
- Offices and shops are visited by an environmental health inspector who is employed by the local authority.
- Fire regulations are enforced by the fire authority.

In all these cases, if working practices are unsatisfactory, an **improvement notice** is issued. This tells the employer exactly what action must be taken and gives a deadline. If working practices are so bad that either the workers or the public are at serious risk, a **prohibition notice** is issued. The employer must stop operations immediately. Employers can appeal if they think a decision is unfair, but if they lose the appeal and still fail to put the matter right, the organisation can be fined or the owner imprisoned.

> One of the highest fines was awarded for a prosecution brought by Basingstoke and Deane Borough Council, in Hampshire, which resulted in a total of £425,000 for six breaches of health and safety law. In February 2001 Doncaster Borough Council was fined £400,000 and ordered to pay £30,000 costs after an electrician was electrocuted at its headquarters because he had never been warned about the exposed wires in a false ceiling.

Act or Regulation	Number of convictions	% of total	Total fines (£)	Average fine per conviction (£)
Health and Safety at Work Act	186		797,089	
Management of Health and Safety at Work Regulations	65		409,064	
Workplace (Health, Safety and Welfare Regulations	24	26,000		
RIDDOR	11		6,500	
Electricity at Work Regulations	19		17,450	
PUWER	19		97,383	
Other legislation or regulations	13		27,658	
Total				

(*Adapted from HSE statistics*)
Convictions and fines in Britain in 1998/99 under HASAWA

Note Your library may have updated figures available when you are doing this task, so you can find out if convictions and/or fines have increased or decreased since the time this table was published.

Test your knowledge and understanding

1   Look at the regulations on pages 52–56 and in the chart on page 57. As a group, suggest which regulations would most apply to the following types of employees:

   a   a hairdresser
   b   an electrician
   c   a word processor operator
   d   a caretaker.

2   The chart on page 58 shows the total number of convictions and fines in Great Britain in 1998/99 under HASWA and the main regulations.

   Use this to answer the questions that follow. If you are taking your Key Skills Application of Number award, keep your answers safely as your work can contribute to your evidence.

   a   Copy out the table, enter all the figures and check you have done this accurately.
   b   Calculate the total number of convictions in 1998/99.
   c   Calculate the total amount of fines.
   d   For each Act or Regulation, calculate the *average* fine per conviction. Round your answer so it is given as a whole number of pounds.
   e   Now find the average total amount (in your bottom right hand box).
   f   In 1997/98, the total average fine was £2,224. From your calculations state:
       i   whether this amount increased in 1998/99
       ii   the percentage change between the two years.
       State whether you think it is good for fines to increase or not – and why.
   g   For each Act or Regulation, work out the percentage number of convictions. Round your answer so you have a whole number and enter this in column 3. Use your answers to help you to construct a pie chart which clearly shows this information. Remember you will have to add a key, so that readers can understand the Act or Regulation represented by each wedge.
   h   As a group, suggest *two* types of offences which could occur under *each* Act or Regulation listed.

Hazards in your workplace

A hazard is anything which could cause you harm. So dozens of everyday objects are hazards – a computer, television, car, knife, icy path – and so on.

The likelihood of an accident happening, or someone being hurt or injured, is the **risk factor**. The risk is higher if:

- the person is untrained
- the item or activity is potentially dangerous
- the person is careless, silly or distracted.

If a risk exists, then:

- it must be assessed as high, medium or low
- where possible the risk must be eliminated or minimised
- if the risk cannot be eliminated, there must be suitable signs to warn people. In some cases, special training for staff may need to be provided.

As a simple example, a clean dry floor is not a hazard. A wet one is. If a customer spilt a bottle of liquid in a supermarket then the staff would:

a immediately screen off the area

b put up a warning notice

c mop up the spillage

d only remove the warning when the area was dry.

In other words, when the risk is 'high' it is minimised and people are warned.

Many of the Regulations listed on page 57 have been introduced to minimise risk. In addition, under the Management of Health and Safety at Work Regulations all employers must undertake regular risk assessments on their premises. This means both identifying hazards and the degree of risk. However, all staff must take action if they spot a hazard.

Health and safety risks in your own job role and taking precautions

There are many potential hazards in an office. These are discussed in more detail on pages 67–68.

Remember, however, that for every potential hazard you identify the risk may be high, medium, low or non-existent. For instance, for equipment and machinery, it depends upon:

- the state of the equipment
- what it does
- how often it is used
- the skills of the user.

Evaluating risks

A risk is high if there is a strong likelihood that people could be hurt or injured because of a hazard. In this case, something must be done to get rid of the hazard or to protect people – as you have seen.

Sensible precautions

These include:

- not attempting anything which is high risk – report it instead
- reading any instruction manuals before you start
- not attempting any potentially hazardous job without proper training
- heeding *all* basic safety precautions, such as disconnecting equipment and machinery from the power source before you clean or move it
- observing all the Regulations you have just read about
- concentrating when you are doing a job
- only doing one job at a time.

Remaining alert to hazards and reporting risks

Even if there are no hazards at your workplace today, the situation could change tomorrow. If it freezes tonight, the steps to an office may be icy in the morning. If the caretaker leaves a large pile of boxes outside your office door, they are a hazard because you have to climb over or round them to get in. Even if your photocopier is working well this afternoon, there is nothing to stop smoke coming from the plug tomorrow morning – and so on!

It is particularly important to be watchful in relation to hazards with a potentially high risk factor, as action needs taking immediately. All the examples you have just read are potentially high risk, so you should:

- ask the caretaker or someone else to put sand or salt on the steps – before someone slips
- get the boxes moved – before someone falls over them
- unplug the photocopier *immediately* and put a notice on it to prevent anyone else plugging it back in again. Then tell your supervisor who will probably want you to phone the technician.

Your actions, in all these cases, will have contributed to preventing an injury or accident to other people.

Requirements and guidance on precautions

All equipment and machinery is sold with a user's handbook. These give the basic facts in relation to the safe working and operation of the item.

In addition, all organisations provide health and safety training and produce a health and safety manual which gives guidance on the precautions you should take before you do any job. This will supplement any specific training you received during induction.

Test your knowledge and understanding

Try your hand at risk assessment by reading the scenario below and answering the supervisor's questions.

Gareth has decided that his filing cabinet would be better if it was positioned at the other side of his desk. Rather than ask for help, he decides to empty it and move it himself. If he has a problem, he thinks he could ask Fatima from the next office to help.

Ten minutes later, he has a pile of files on his desk and is just about to pull and shove the filing cabinet into position when his supervisor walks in. In horror, she asks Gareth to evaluate the risks involved in doing this.

When Gareth looks blank, his supervisor tells him a decision can only be made when he has assessed:

- the task
- the load
- the environment
- his own capability.

Test your knowledge and understanding *continued*

- **The task.** The job involves manual handling if it is concerned with any of the following. Identify all those that apply:

  pushing, pulling, lifting, lowering, twisting, turning, carrying or team lifting.

- **The load.** This relates to the object to be moved. Identify all that apply:

  heavy, slippery, difficult or awkward to hold, sharp, unstable, bulky.

- **The workplace environment.** Identify all that apply:

  confined space, very hot or cold, movement between floor levels, uneven or slippery floor.

- **The individual's capability.** Identify all that apply:

  Has Gareth received training on manual handling techniques, is extra strength or height required, is extra help available, are women expected to be involved or young people under 18?

1 Do you still think Gareth should move the filing cabinet on his own? Give a reason for your answer.

2 Risk assessment probably involves more factors than you perhaps thought at first.
   a Identify one type of load which you could move safely on your own. Describe it in terms of the task, type of load, environment and in relation to your own capability.
   b Identify one type of load which two of you, working together, must not move because the risk would be too high. Again, describe it in terms of the task, type of load and environment – as well as your own abilities.

Identify the hazards and evaluate the risks in your workplace

All organisations have policies to help to reduce or control hazards and to try to prevent accidents. These policies, and the people responsible for health and safety in your workplace, are covered in this section. You will also gain further practice in identifying hazards, evaluating risks and see how to report these.

Workplace policies for controlling risks

All organisations must comply with health and safety laws and must be able to prove that they do so. Therefore they have policies – or plans of action – which show what they have done and what they have asked their employees to do.

The documents and systems in place are likely to include:

- a **safety policy** which states the aims of the organisation in relation to the health and safety of its employees. This is a legal requirement. Members of staff responsible for health and safety will also be listed in addition to:
  - arrangements for training and instruction
  - company rules
  - emergency arrangements
  - how accidents are reported
  - how risk areas are identified.

  This document is signed by a senior manager and kept up-to-date.
- **codes of practice** which tell all employees what to do in an emergency, such as a fire, gas leak or bomb scare. They also include what to do if an accident occurs (see opposite).
- a **safety committee** operates in many large organisations. Both management and employees may be members. There may also be **safety representatives** who attend meetings of this committee. Some organisations employ a **safety officer** either as well, or instead of, a safety committee. Their responsibilities include:
  - checking health and safety laws are being kept
  - reporting any new hazards
  - reporting any breaches of safety regulations
  - following up employee complaints
  - checking accident trends and reports
  - advising on safety matters in general.

In addition, the employer will consult either the safety committee or safety officer about any proposed changes which may affect health and safety or about any training planned for staff.

Accident reporting

All organisations have a system for reporting and recording accidents to comply with RIDDOR regulations (see page 57). If there are more than 10 employees an accident book must be kept and all records stored for at least 3 years. In most cases 'near-misses' are also logged, so that areas for improvement can be identified.

If you witness an accident or are involved in one, you will have to complete an accident report form. If the accident is serious, it will be investigated by the safety officer or a safety representative and nothing must be moved or changed until this has been done.

An accident book

Evidence collection

1   Obtain copies of workplace policies and other documents produced by your employer which relate to health and safety in your job. This could be in your full-time job or, if you are a student, in a job you do on a part-time basis. Remember that you may have been given some of these during your induction. List these clearly and state how they affect you when you are doing your work.

    If you are a full-time student, the same principles apply. You will have to abide by college health and safety regulations, so you need a copy of these and then say how they affect your work and behaviour.

2   List the people who are responsible for health and safety in your workplace or your college and say where they are located. In addition, say who you would contact in an emergency and why you would choose this person.

3   Write down the information you were given in induction when you were told what to do in an emergency, such as:
    –   an emergency evacuation
    –   if you witnessed an accident
    –   if you had an accident yourself.

Check it out!

1 Obtain a copy of an accident report form from your employer or college. Check the type of information you would be asked for and how you must fill it in. Find out the name of the person who would receive the completed form.

2 Check you would know what to do if your friend tripped over a loose tile in the office and twisted his ankle so badly he couldn't walk. In particular, write down:

- how you would contact a first aider
- where the nearest medical room is
- under what circumstances you could summon a doctor or send for an ambulance
- what information you would put on the accident form as a witness to the event.

Responsibilities for health and safety in your job description and reporting health and safety matters

Your **job description** summarises all the main responsibilities that you have at work – usually in the form of a list of the tasks or jobs you must do. If you worked as a health and safety officer, *all* your job would be concerned with health and safety. If you worked for the health and safety officer you may have some specific tasks to do relating to health and safety. As an administrator in another area you may find there are a few general sentences relating to health and safety such as:

- to comply with the safety policy of the organisation
- to use recommended working practices
- to identify and evaluate risks relating to your own job role
- to report such risks and problems promptly to the correct person.

To be able to comply with these requirements you have to:

- know the documents your employer has prepared relating to health and safety – in particular, written procedures which say how you must do your job
- be able to identify potential hazards in your job
- be able to identify any aspects of the workplace which could harm yourself or other people, such as your colleagues, customers, visitors, students or contractors who are working on the premises
- decide the risk factor for these hazards and:
  - report those with a high factor to a responsible person

– deal with those hazards with a low risk factor according to your workplace policies and the law on health and safety.

The potential hazards and risks in your job

The hazards and risks relating to your job can be divided into the following categories:

- the use and maintenance of machinery and equipment
- the use of materials and substances
- unsafe working practices – or those which go against company policies
- unsafe behaviour
- accidental breakages and spillages
- environmental factors.

For each of these categories there are certain points to consider and a range of *potential* hazards. Before you can start to evaluate the possible risk, look at the table on page 68 which summarises these.

Test your knowledge and understanding

1   Work through the table on page 68, preferably in a group. Decide which hazards you think are likely to be:

   a   a high risk and should be reported immediately to a person responsible for health and safety

   b   not a particularly high risk, but should be reported because you cannot remedy the problem yourself

   c   a low risk and you can deal with them yourself (either by changing your behaviour or taking a simple action).

   Discuss your suggestions with your tutor.

2   As you go through this list, think about ways in which risks could be put right. Then keep your suggestions safely and check them when you have finished reading the next section.

3   When a risk cannot be eliminated, warning signs must be put up. These are:
   - red for a prohibited (forbidden) action,
   - blue for a mandatory (must do) action and
   - green for a safe condition.

   Find *at least* one example of each of these coloured signs in your workplace or college. In each case explain why it is that particular colour. Compare your list with others in your group to see how many different signs you have spotted altogether.

Category	Main considerations	Potential hazards
Machinery and equipment	Usage Maintenance and cleaning Staff training Repairing of faults	Ozone fumes from photocopier or laser printer Toner in photocopier or laser printer chemicals Watching ultraviolet light when photocopying Touching hot, sharp surfaces inside photocopier Noise from copier, printer or fax Faulty wiring or plugs or trailing wires or incorrect fuse fitted No routine maintenance policy
Materials and substances	Handling Storage Disposal	Unlabelled bottles of substances Not replacing top or cap on substances or correcting fluids Getting toner powder on skin or in eyes Breathing toxic fumes Not disposing of dangerous substances properly
Unsafe working practices	Emergency procedures Manual handling Computer use Personal protective equipment Manuals/instructions	Ignoring fire alarm or disregarding proper procedure to use escape routes or go to assembly point Lifting heavy, bulky, unstable loads Ignoring breaks, poor workstation design Not using PPE when told to do so (e.g. rubber gloves, hard hat, goggles etc.) Not reading instructions, not reporting faults
Unsafe behaviour	Rushing and running Practical jokes 'Bad' housekeeping, untidiness or sloppy habits Stupidity	Bumping into other people or falling over Dangers to other people Leaving drawers open, stacking up files on a shelf, using basic items (scissors, knives, stapler) without care, not mopping up spills Using water to clean electrical equipment
Environmental factors	Ventilation/temperature and clean air Space to work safely Noise Lighting Building requirements Rest rooms/welfare	Heating broken, no window blinds, sealed windows but no air-conditioning, no policy on smoking, over-crowding of staff Traffic noise, telephones/printers Poor natural light, drab paintwork, dirty or insufficient lights or lights not over desks Faulty rails on stairs or landings, no viewing panels in two-way doors, slippery or wet floors Insufficient toilets and washing facilities

Potential hazards and risks at work

Information update

The Trades Union Congress (TUC) is very concerned about the accident rate for young workers. In an average week, ten workers aged between 15 and 24 are seriously injured at work. One in three young people also receives no health and safety training – even though this is illegal.

The TUC have issued a leaflet *Play it Safe at Work* which you can get from a careers adviser, from the National Union of Students or direct from the TUC by ringing them on 0870 600 4882. You can also download it from their website at www.tuc.org.uk.

Evidence collection

Assess your own workplace or method of working.

1   Start by identifying any working practices that you do or which relate to your job which could harm yourself or anyone else.

2   Identify any other aspects of the workplace which *could* harm yourself or other people (including visitors).

3   Select at least two of the following types of hazards or risks in your workplace or college to investigate further:

    a   the use and maintenance or machinery or equipment

    b   the use of materials or substances

    c   working practices that do not conform to (match) laid down policies

    d   unsafe behaviour

    e   accidental breakages or spillages

    f   environmental factors.

    For the two that you have chosen, decide which are:

        i   the highest risk to yourself or others and should be reported to someone

        ii   low risk and could be dealt with according to workplace policies and legal requirements.

4   Finally, expect your assessor to talk to you about what you would do if you were investigating a hazard or risk relating to the other types listed above.

Reduce the risks to health and safety in your workplace

You only reduce risks if you take action. One way of doing this is to report a problem – or someone behaving irresponsibly – to your line manager or supervisor. The second is to take action yourself by reducing or eliminating the risk.

You have already learned how to evaluate a risk. Now you have to learn what action you can take yourself – quite safely – to put matters right.

Workplace policies covering your job role

Quite obviously, if you are working safely, you should know the workplace policies which relate to your job role and *follow them*. These will have been devised with your safety – and legal requirements – in mind. They will vary, depending upon your specific duties, but are likely to cover areas such as:

● how to work and use equipment safely

● how to use hazardous substances

● organisational rules relating to smoking, eating, drinking (alcohol) and drugs

● the action to take in an emergency

● your personal presentation and personal conduct.

Do note that your workplace policies may not have the same titles as the list above. You may, for instance, have guidelines on computer use – in which case this relates to using equipment.

Suppliers' and manufacturers' instructions

Suppliers and manufacturers issue instructions – and sometimes quite complicated handbooks – with the equipment they sell. In addition, if you buy a wide range of stationery products and materials – from paper to a printer cartridge – you are likely to find instructions printed on the packet or on a leaflet inside.

It is always tempting to ignore the box, the leaflet or the manual and just unpack and use the item you have bought. This is not very important with a packet of paper but with other products, such as a toxic or inflammable cleaning solution, you should be far more careful. Often quite common items have some unexpected notes and requirements! Did you know, for instance, that you shouldn't use a telephone where the receiver is linked to the base unit (or fax or answering machine) in a lightning storm?

Stop worrying – he's read the manual!

Evidence collection

1   Obtain a copy of the most recent workplace policies for your job role – or which apply to you as a student. Write a brief summary which states how these affect you when you are working. If possible you should check that you obtain policies relating to at least four of the following:

   a   the use of safe working methods and equipment

   b   the safe use of hazardous substances

   c   smoking, eating, drinking and drugs

   d   what to do in an emergency

   e   personal presentation and the wearing of personal protective equipment.

2   Obtain manufacturer's or supplier's instructions you need or have read as part of your work (either in the workplace or in a college office).

   a   State why you found these helpful and when you have used them – or might need to use them.

   b   Explain how you use them to make sure you use equipment, materials and products safely.

   c   If you find there are any differences between these and your workplaces policies state the person to whom you would report the matter.

Information update

People don't just stay away from work because they have an accident or are physically ill. In one survey of offices, 28% of people were off work through stress-related illnesses. Another reason for absence is dislike of a job – or fear. Some employees in 'vulnerable' occupations, such as benefit offices and housing departments, have been worried about violence from callers.

The most common cause of workplace stress is feeling you have no control over what is happening to you. You may have too much (or too little) work to do, have to work long hours, your work may be boring, your boss may be very critical. Rather than stay at home because you cannot cope, it is much better to talk to someone in confidence. Choose someone you trust at work, your tutor or a specialist counsellor at college. This will help you feel better and is the first step towards taking back some control over your life.

Violence at work must obviously be avoided at all costs. Most organisations have procedures which staff must follow if they feel threatened. In jobs where this might happen, staff are usually protected by glass screens and have a panic button under the counter which they can press to summon immediate help. Never try to 'brazen out' a difficult situation. If you can't cope with someone, get help quickly – before the problem gets worse.

Safe working practices for your own job role

You have read a lot about hazards and risks in this unit. This section now concentrates on safe working behaviour in your own job role.

There are normally three ways of doing most jobs in relation to safety:

- the best way – which is the least risky
- the luckiest way – which is risky, but this time you get away with it
- the hard, careless or sloppy way – which can have serious consequences. Sooner or later you will have an accident.

The table on the page opposite shows the actions you should take in relation to all the main areas related to administration. Read this carefully and then extend your knowledge and understanding by doing the quiz on page 74.

REDUCING RISKS BY WORKING SAFELY

Safe working methods

Do as you are told (whether you agree or not!).
Don't run up and down stairs, along corridors and around corners.
Don't carry high loads so you can't see over the top or lift heavy weights.
Follow all recommended working practices relating to your computer.
Close drawers immediately after use and keep your working area tidy.
Put rubbish in the right container and wrap broken glass before putting it in the bin.
Stack items safely – not so they overbalance. Use protective clothing and equipment when you should. Use the correct equipment for the job and concentrate whilst you are working. Report faults and hazards promptly.

Using equipment safely

Refer to the manufacturer's handbook for any queries. If you don't understand what is meant, or if the entry is different from your workplace policies, tell your supervisor. Tell your supervisor also if you think any equipment isn't positioned, used or maintained in accordance with manufacturer's/supplier's instructions.
Wear rubber gloves when changing toner cartridges and *don't* shake them. If you get toner powder on skin wash off immediately with cold water.
Close the lid when photocopying and don't poke about inside or touch anything inside.
Switch off a machine if you smell overheating, burning or smoke and report immediately.
Switch off machines when instructed to do so.
Only clean machines and equipment using the recommended products and procedure as stated in the handbook. Never use equipment you are not trained to operate or which is labelled 'faulty'.

Using hazardous substances safely

Read the label or leaflet before you open the lid. Don't breathe the fumes.
Fasten securely immediately after use. Return to proper storage area – this should be a cool place away from naked lights and fires. Dispose of empty containers according to instructions.

Smoking, eating, drinking and drugs

Follow your employer's policies on smoking and drinking (alcohol) or expect to be disciplined.
Normally smoking is prohibited in office areas and alcohol is not allowed on the premises.
Drinking alcohol at lunchtime is also discouraged or forbidden.
Don't bring food with spices or a strong odour to work (e.g. hard-boiled eggs and garlic bread), especially if it is customary to eat at your desk. If there is a separate eating area, use it.
Keep soft drinks well away from electrical equipment and your computer keyboard. Mop up spills immediately.
If you are prescribed medication to take at work by your doctor, tell your supervisor.
Expect your employer to take serious disciplinary action against anyone who handles or takes harmful or illegal substances into the workplace.

In the case of an emergency

Immediately follow the correct procedure, no matter how inconvenient!
In a bomb alert, take your belongings with you; in a fire alert, leave them behind unless they are next to you.
If you see smoke, sound the fire alarm. If you smell gas or see a water leak, tell a senior person immediately.
If you work in the mailroom, check the procedures for receiving suspicious packages.
Learn first aid – then you can help people who choke, faint or suffer an electric shock.
Your training could save someone's life.

Test your knowledge and understanding

1   Suggest the best action to take in each of the following situations. Discuss your ideas with your tutor. Suggested answers are on page 227.

   a   The front door of the photocopier swings open and refuses to close properly when you are in the middle of an important job.

   b   You are desperate to open a window and can't find the safety stool.

   c   The electricians arrive to check all the portable electrical equipment. They put stickers on all those they have checked. Afterwards you remember there are two more laptop computers.

   d   A team member is urgently trying to finish a long, important and difficult piece of work. She has had few breaks and taken lunch at her desk. Five minutes ago she burst into tears and said she couldn't cope any longer.

   e   You are getting solvent out of the cupboard to give to the caretaker who needs it to clean some graffiti off the wall outside. The top is loose and you spill some of the solution over your hand and arm.

   f   When you plug in a fan heater on a cold day the plug goes 'pop'.

2   According to a survey by the law firm Eversheds, 80% of employers have had to deal with employees consuming alcohol at work and 17% have had experience of employees taking drugs at work. Discuss with your supervisor or tutor what you would do if you saw a member of your team either drinking alcohol or taking drugs in the workplace.

Information update

Working environments are safer today than they have ever been. The result is in the reduction in accidents and injuries in the workplace over the last ten years. However, whilst some types of injuries have decreased, others have increased. These include aching arms and hands, swollen fingers, painful wrists, backache, a stiff neck, sore eyes, headaches and even migraines. Why is this?

According to the European Agency for Safety and Health at Work, up to 50% of all work-related sickness today is caused by **musculoskeletal disorders**. This is a term used for a variety of problems which affect your muscles and joints. You may have heard this called **repetitive strain injury**. This results in pain and swelling or 'pins and needles' in the hands and wrists and is caused by repetitive movements. It is experienced by a wide variety of workers including musicians, packers and computer users who do a lot of keyboarding. Changing your keyboard for a mouse doesn't help very much – as again you keep repeating the same movements. The correct term, however, is **upper limb disorders** as the symptoms affect the hands, wrists, arms, elbows, shoulders or neck.

The two main reasons for this problem occurring are:

- sitting in the same position for hours and hours every day
- stress and pressure to do a job quickly and accurately.

Another problem is the telephone. Office workers are apt to answer the phone and wedge it between their shoulder and neck so that they can carry on typing. A handful of people have even died from doing this! If you use a phone regularly as part of your job, you should wear a headset.

There is a right way and a wrong way to answer the telephone

If you are interested in finding out more and have Internet access, a good website to try is www.repetitive-strain-injury.com/

Action to take

You already know that, according to the law:

- your workstation and VDU must be assessed
- you must take regular breaks
- you can have free eyesight tests
- the lighting and humidity must be appropriate
- you should have health and safety training.

However, you should take appropriate action yourself. Therefore:

- check your furniture meets the regulations
- sit properly
- stretch every 15 minutes – stop typing and file some papers instead
- investigate products such as split keyboards, ergonomic keyboards and a trackball
- rest, flex and exercise your wrists regularly – ask for a wrist rest if you need one.

Test your knowledge and understanding

Assess yourself and evaluate your own risks in relation to using a computer. Do this by answering the questions below. In each case select the option which you think is correct and check your answers with those given on page 227.

1   Musculoskeletal disorders are made worse by:
    a   poorly laid out workstations
    b   changing activity often
    c   walking around regularly.

2   Headaches and visual problems are made worse if:
    a   there are blinds at the windows
    b   there is a reflection on the screen
    c   the computer user wears glasses.

3   Risks to computer operators can be reduced by:
    a   proper training
    b   ergonomic keyboards
    c   both of these.

4   A 'discretionary break' is
    a   time off for lunch
    b   a break when the person feels it is necessary
    c   a change of activity.

5   Your keyboard should be:
    a   attached to the equipment
    b   set at an angle
    c   easily readable.

6   Your sitting posture should be such that you are:
    a   sitting up straight with your back supported
    b   leaning forwards
    c   leaning back.

7   You should have been trained to:
    a   recognise risks, sit properly and take breaks
    b   adjust your equipment, clean your screen, use your computer system
    c   do all of these.

- never use a laptop for longer than necessary and have frequent breaks if you are using it where you can't sit properly
- position your VDU so it isn't in front of a blank wall – it is better in front of a window so you can look out regularly (this exercises your eye muscles)
- blink regularly
- drink plenty of water
- adjust the screen so it suits you and glare is minimised
- if you are offered an eye test – take one!

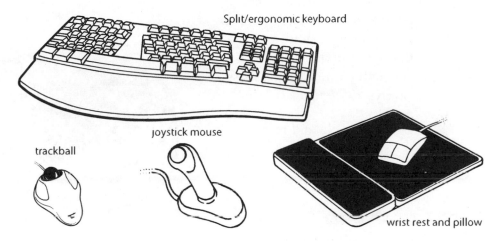

These devices can help to make the working environment safer

Personal presentation and personal conduct

Your personal presentation relates to your appearance and your personal conduct relates to how you act on a day-to-day basis – not just on special occasions or when your boss is around!

Personal presentation

In many jobs there are regulations relating to dress – often known as the **dress code**. As an administrator you are expected to use your common sense and to dress suitably for your job.

- Wear appropriate clothes. Very few organisations allow office staff to wear jeans, T-shirts and trainers. If you are female, avoid tight, short skirts which make it difficult to move around.
- Remove dangling jewellery if you operate equipment and tie back long hair – or remove your tie – before you lean over the shredder.
- Wear sensible footwear. Very high heels and 'clumpy' shoes should be avoided as they make you unsteady on your feet.

- Wear an overall if you are doing a dirty job, to protect your clothes. If you need to use protective equipment then do so – no matter what you look like!
- Be 'nice to be near' because you are vigilant about personal freshness and never eating highly flavoured foods (or garlic) when you are working. If you do, invest in a good breath freshener and use it!

Personal conduct

Your personal conduct relates to your everyday behaviour and attitude towards other people. Accidents are often caused through a moment's lack of concentration or carelessness. Always *think first*, act later.

Being sensible and responsible doesn't mean you will become a boring person. Many very sensible people are full of fun and great to know. They just don't take risks which are unacceptable.

Information update

Psychologists have recently identified people who are more accident prone than others. Apparently, you are more likely to have an accident or be injured if you are: imaginative, open-minded, aggressive, selfish, irresponsible, unhelpful, rebellious or not very conscientious.

All of these may be understandable apart from 'imaginative' and 'open-minded'. However, the reason is because you are more likely to try to multi-task and do too many things at once. A typical example is a driver rushing to a business appointment and checking the map, answering the phone and driving at the same time!

Check it out!

Check how responsible you are by seeing how many of the following statements you can answer 'Yes' to (honestly)!

1 You don't act differently when your boss or tutor has left the room.

2 You are generally neat and tidy.

3 You care about other people and try to talk them out of doing something silly.

4 You are prepared to ask for help if you don't understand something.

5 You follow instructions carefully.

6 You take your time if the job is difficult.

7 You always clean up afterwards if a job has been messy.

8 If you say you will do something, you do it.

9 You like helping other people.

10 You don't take unacceptable risks.

Evidence collection

1 Explain how you make sure your personal conduct never endangers the health and safety of yourself or anyone else.

2 Describe how you make sure your personal presentation at work ensures the health and safety of yourself and others, meets any legal duties and is in accordance with workplace policies.

3 If possible, obtain witness testimony from your supervisor or tutor which confirms that your personal conduct and presentation is always appropriate and in accordance with all health and safety requirements.

Your scope and responsibility in putting right risks

By now, you should be quite an expert at:

- identifying hazards
- assessing risks
- deciding what to do.

The danger, however, is that you become over-confident and start to do more than you should!

You can put risks right yourself if they relate to:

- your own workstation or working area
- your own working methods or working practices
- your personal presentation or personal conduct.

As a first step, know and accept your own limitations, otherwise you will take risks you shouldn't.

Workplace procedures for handling risks you are unable to deal with

There will be workplace policies and procedures which not only say how risks should be handled but who should deal with them. You should check them to find out:

- the type of risks which are listed in them
- who to contact if you identify these types of risks.

If you work in a large organisation, you will find there are a number of internal staff you can contact from other departments, such as:

- an estates department, which deals with general building repairs
- an electrical section, which deals with electrical faults
- a computer services section, which deals with computer problems
- caretakers or janitors who will help you over general problems such as a leak
- cleaners who will remove rubbish and help to tidy up an area if there has been a serious spillage or problem
- security staff you can call on if you feel intimidated or threatened.

In a small office, you will have to notify your supervisor or line manager who will decide whether external assistance is required.

Check it out!

For each of the following situations:

a say whether the risk factor is high or low.

b find out the person to whom you should report each hazard in either your college or your workplace. If you work part-time as well as attending college, find out who you would report to and what you should do both at work and at college.

c say what action you would take yourself, where appropriate, to prevent further problems until your specialist person arrived.

   1 Someone slams a door and the glass cracks.

   2 You break a glass container.

   3 The heating won't work in the middle of winter.

   4 The shredder jams.

   5 You notice a shelf full of files is loose on the wall.

   6 The fluorescent tube above your desk starts to flicker.

   7 You knock an open (and full) bottle of correcting fluid over your computer keyboard.

Test your knowledge and understanding

If you are doing your Key Skills Application of Number award this final exercise will contribute towards your evidence.

Study the table on page 82. This gives the injuries experienced by office staff during 1998/9 by category.

1 Copy out this table and enter all the figures neatly and correctly.

2 The accidents are by category, and also divided into major injuries and those which were less major but led to more than 3 days' absence. Calculate the total number of major injuries and the total number of over 3 day injuries.

3 Work out the percentage for each type of category in both columns. Remember you are dealing with people, so your answers must be in whole numbers.

4 Calculate the total number of injuries, regardless of whether they were major or over 3 day, for all categories.

5 Use your totals from (4) above to construct a bar chart, which clearly shows which type of injuries and accidents are the most common. Decide a suitable scale or proportion for each of your bars.

6 From your analyses of the figures in the table, what precautions do you think are the most important in an office to prevent common injuries and accidents occurring? Support your ideas with information you have obtained from working with these statistics.

7 Read the scenario below and then carry out the task which follows.

Sam Wright is the new sales officer at Ramsey Engineering. The company has been in business for nearly 50 years making special orders for a large number of customers all over the UK.

Sam decides to investigate long term accident trends so that he can gain a better picture of the company. Fortunately the records have been carefully filed for all employees who have been absent for 3 days or more. He obtains the figures for every 5 years since 1975 and lists these by type of employee.

1975	Production 17%	Administrators 11%	Sales reps 5%
1980	Production 16%	Administrators 10%	Sales reps 6%
1985	Production 14%	Administrators 9%	Sales reps 7%
1990	Production 11%	Administrators 9%	Sales reps 10%
1995	Production 10%	Administrators 10%	Sales reps 11%
2000	Production 9%	Administrators 9%	Sales reps 12%

a Create a line graph entitled 'Percentage of accidents by type of employee 1975–2000'. Use the information given to draw three graphs on the same sheet of paper.

b What trends do you notice? Can you suggest any reason for these?

Type of accident	Major		Over 3 days		Total accidents
	Number	%	Number	%	
Contact with moving machinery	1		18		
Struck by moving object	22		182		
Struck by moving vehicle	3		25		
Strike against something fixed	17		82		
Handling, lifting or carrying	34		396		
Slip or trip	199		381		
Falls from a height	56		94		
Trapped by something collapsing/overturning	3		21		
Contact with a harmful substance	2		26		
Act of violence	16		46		
Other	8		61		
Total					

(Adapted from HSE statistics)

Injuries to employees in offices by kind of accident and severity of injury, 1998/99

Evidence collection

1   If you have made any suggestions for reducing risks in your workplace or college, or have put right any risks yourself, write a description of what happened and what you did. Ask your supervisor or tutor to countersign your account.

2   Similarly, if you have been involved in taking action in an emergency, write a short report about what you did and ask your supervisor or tutor to countersign it.

3   Prove that you have followed workplace policies for at least *four* of the following:

   a   the use of safe working methods and equipment
   b   the safe use of hazardous substances
   c   smoking, eating, drinking and drugs
   d   what to do in an emergency
   e   personal presentation.

   Do this by explaining:

   ●   what the policy says you must do (or attaching a copy as evidence)
   ●   what actions you have taken to make sure you are following the policy.

   Be as specific as possible. For instance, refer to a particular piece of equipment, or how you handle a certain substance.

   Ask your supervisor or tutor to countersign your account.

   Finally, expect your assessor to talk to you about how you would follow workplace policies for the remaining item.

Prepare and copy routine documents

This unit is concerned with how to:

- prepare routine documents
- photocopy routine documents.

It is **important** because:

- many documents are prepared in offices every day
- you need to know how to produce simple documents for other members of staff
- you will often be asked to make copies of documents you have received and prepared
- the most common method of making copies is to use a photocopier – in virtually every workplace.

There are two elements to this unit. Before you start these you need to check that you understand the health and safety requirements in relation to preparing and copying documents, why documents are often required by a set deadline and why it is important to tell people if you cannot meet this deadline.

Key skills signpost

As you progress through this unit, you can also develop your skills to produce evidence towards the Key Skills Unit in Information Technology at level 1. This is because the vast majority of documents prepared today are created using a computer.

You have been given two tasks. These are:

1. To prepare an information sheet for staff on the computer supplies that are available from your computer services staff shop. Your boss, Eileen Pickford, has also asked you to find out information about the prices of these, so she can check she is paying the right price.

2. To prepare a simple safety guide for users of *either* computer equipment *or* the photocopying machine.

IT1.1

For task 1:

Find out the cost of the following computer supplies in your area.

- cordless mouse (state the make you have chosen)
- ergonomic keyboard (again, state the make you have chosen)
- HP Deskjet cartridge – black for a 690C ink jet printer
- HP Laserjet 5000 toner
- box of 10 3.5″ floppy disks for IBM computer
- mousemat
- wrist rest
- screen clean wipes
- aerosol duster for cleaning keyboards
- footrest
- computer VDU filter.

Do this by:

a surfing the Internet (sites to try include www.pcworld.co.uk and www.globaldirect.co.uk)

b looking at catalogues and price lists from large or local suppliers, such as Staples superstores.

For task 2:

a Obtain the manufacturer's handbook for the equipment you have chosen from your supervisor or tutor and note down any important information you need.

b Find out if your manufacturer has a website you can access for more information. Or access the HSE site on www.open.gov.uk/hsehome.htm to see what you can find which is relevant.

c Visit your library to look at additional information which is available in books or on CD-Roms.

IT1.2

For task 1

Use the information you have obtained on computer supplies to prepare a table for your boss which identifies each item and gives the average price.

Prepare a draft page to advertise the items to staff. Use clip-art or other images to illustrate the page effectively. At this stage, do not include any prices. Head it 'Computer Supplies Staff Shop'.

Prepare a short memo which simply explains what you have done and to which you can attach the table and your draft advertisement. Mention that you will obviously amend this to include prices when Eileen confirms these.

Save your work carefully so that it will be easy to update.

For task 2

Prepare a draft safety guide which can be put on noticeboards near the equipment. Do not exceed three pages and make sure it is clear to see and read. Where possible use images or clip-art to illustrate important points.

When you have completed the draft, save it carefully. Then ask your tutor or supervisor for comments. Make any corrections or changes that are required to incorporate their suggestions and then take a print-out of the final version.

Prepare and copy routine documents

A routine document is a standard document which is frequently required and is therefore needed more often than other types.

To make copies of routine documents you have to set your printer to print multiple copies – or use the photocopier. Unless you have a very high speed printer then it is always sensible to take a large number of copies on a photocopier.

Health and safety requirements

This unit covers health and safety requirements when using a keyboard and when using a photocopier.

If you have just completed unit 102, then you should already know a considerable amount about both of these. However, to make sure they are clear, the main points about keyboarding are summarised in the table on the next page. The main health and safety requirements in relation to photocopiers are dealt with in the next element.

Check it out!

Read through the table on the next page and check that you understand all the points that are made about using keyboards safely. Look in a stationery catalogue, around your local PC World superstore or on the Internet (eg www.pcworld.co.uk) to see the range of ergonomic keyboards, wrist rests and trackballs available.

Producing the document on time

In unit 101 you learned about deadlines and that if you couldn't meet a deadline it was very important to tell the right person in good time for alternative action to be taken.

Keyboards: health and safety requirements

- Learn to keyboard *properly*, don't 'hunt and peck'. You will not only work more quickly, but also more safely because your posture will be better.

- Check your overall posture – feet should be on the floor, your legs or ankles shouldn't be crossed, your arms slightly sloping downwards. Sit on a proper, adjustable chair with your back supported. Ask for a foot rest if you need one.

- Your keyboard must be separate from your computer and there must be a clear space between the front of your keyboard and the edge of your desk

- If possible, use an ergonomic keyboard.

- Tilt the keyboard at the best angle for yourself using the tiny feet underneath.

- Use a wrist rest or a wrist pillow to distribute your wrist pressure more evenly.

- Keep your keyboard clean – use a pressurised air canister, a small brush or battery powered keyboard vacuum.

- Use a copyholder which holds your copy at eye level so that you don't need to keep bending your head to read and risk straining your neck.

- If you regularly use a mouse, buy a mouse pad which incorporates a wrist rest and which has been ergonomically designed to reduce pressure on your wrist and arm. Check out alternatives to a standard mouse, such as trackballs and other devices.

The keyboard must

☑ be adjustable   ☑ be separate from the computer   ☑ have clear symbols

This is very important in relation to document preparation. Most organisations have a 'final time' for items to be sent to the post. This may be as early as 2 pm – because the mailroom staff need time to prepare all the items they receive.

Internal documents are just as important. Your boss may have promised to send someone a document in time to take it to a customer or before a meeting starts. If you simply don't say anything – but don't send the document as promised – then your boss will appear inefficient and unreliable to other people.

Element 103.1 — Prepare routine documents

There are dozens of different kinds of documents handled at work every day. Some of these are mainly sent externally whilst others are kept within the organisation.

External documents

These are documents sent from the premises to other organisations and individuals. The main routine document is a business letter. Other types include completed forms, fax messages and financial documents such as orders and invoices. E-mails can also be sent externally over the Internet.

Internal documents

These are documents sent from one person or department in an organisation to another. They include documents sent from one branch of a company to another, because this is still the same organisation. The main routine document is a memo. Other types include telephone messages, e-mails, short reports, notices and meeting documents.

You have already seen how to prepare telephone messages in unit 101. In this unit you will learn how to produce:

- a simple information sheet or account of something that happened
- a business letter
- a memo
- an e-mail message.

Checking the original

You will normally receive original documents to type in one of two ways: typescript or handwriting.

A typed document may be one which has been drafted or produced earlier and to which corrections or amendments have been made – usually in writing. If it has been prepared previously on a computer then you should have a copy on a disk which you can access, so you simply make the changes.

Alternatively, some documents will be produced entirely in handwriting.

In both cases you must check, before you start, that you understand:

- how to lay out the document
- all the handwritten notes or handwriting
- any arrows or other marks which indicate you must do something – such as move text around, replace text or delete text.

This saves you time, because you can check all your queries *at one time* with the person who gave you the work.

Checks to make

Check through any document you receive by:

- reading it carefully, word by word
- putting a clear mark (such as a * in red or in pencil) where you have a query
- double checking all names and technical terms (especially the spelling) and all numbers
- checking each text instruction to see if you can follow it
- discussing your queries with the person who gave you the document
- *writing down* the answer to each query. *Never* rely on your memory!

Whatever you do, *never* just guess what has been written.

Laying out routine documents

Some organisations have a specific method of setting out all their business documents. This is called the **house style**. If this applies in any organisation where you work then your life is made easier, as you must follow this layout all the time.

In other organisations, people normally use the same layout and you can check this by looking through one of the files containing business correspondence. There are also certain 'conventions' which are normally followed for routine documents. These are described below.

However, before you start, note the golden rules which apply to **all** documents you type.

Golden rules for all documents

1 You must be consistent throughout one document. This means, for instance that:

- your spacing between paragraphs is always the same
- your spacing after headings is always the same
- your spacing between any columns is the same.

This makes the document look attractive and easy to read.

2 Keep it simple! Today people dislike fancy headings or elaborate layouts.

3 Your finished document must not contain *any* typing errors.

4 No matter what books say (including this one!) about laying out documents, when you are at work you have to set them all out as you are asked by your employer.

Simple information sheets

These are very basic documents which are prepared every day in organisations. The following points should be noted about preparing them.

- There may be one or two headings. The most important heading is the **main heading** and below this there may be a **sub-heading**. It is normal to make the main heading the most important.

> ### CAR PARKING PERMITS
> #### Dyson Watt car park
>
> We have been offered a limited number of car parking permits for the use of the nearby car park on Bridge Road owned by Dyson and Watt. The cost of these is £25 each for the year.
>
> If any staff would like one, please contact Eileen Drury in the Administration Office as soon as possible.
>
> Greg Quinn
> Administration Manager
> 24.3.02

A simple information sheet for internal use

- The text below will be divided into paragraphs. There may also be numbered or bullet points.

- The spacing and layout of the document may often depend on why it is being prepared. A document for a staff notice board, for instance, may be clearer in double line spacing.

- At the end, you will often find the writer's name and, below this, the date the document was created. If the document is internal, the date may be in a shortened form, eg 21.5.03.

Business letters

Business letters tend to follow certain conventions.

- All business letters are written on letter-headed paper – usually just called 'headed paper' for short. This paper has the name of the organisation, its address, fax and phone number, e-mail and web site addresses and company logo on it. Limited companies also put the address of their registered office and their registration number on the bottom.

- In this unit you will only be expected to prepare short documents. However, if a letter comprises more than one page, the second (and subsequent) pages are *not* typed on headed paper. Some organisations have special continuation paper with their name and logo at the top. Most, however, just use plain, good quality paper, such as bond paper.

- The left hand margin of the letter often follows the design of the letter heading and starts at the point at which the printer's left hand margin begins.

- The standard format is called **fully blocked** because every line starts at the left margin.

- Most organisations today use **open punctuation**. This means that you don't put any punctuation in the address, salutation or complimentary close. You just put normal punctuation in the main part (the 'body') of the letter so that the reader can understand it!

Check it out!

Look at the letter on the next page, which has open punctuation, and check through all the key items which are identified with an arrow. Then read the explanations which follow, to make sure you understand exactly how you would type each one.

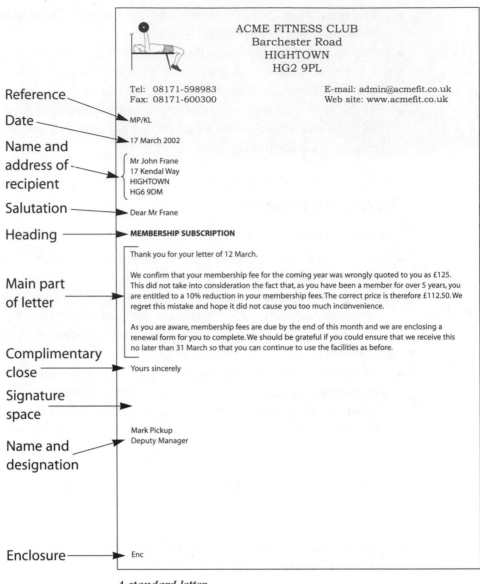

The labels pointing to the letter read:

Reference → MP/KL

Date → 17 March 2002

Name and address of recipient →
Mr John Frane
17 Kendal Way
HIGHTOWN
HG6 9DM

Salutation → Dear Mr Frane

Heading → **MEMBERSHIP SUBSCRIPTION**

Main part of letter →
Thank you for your letter of 12 March.

We confirm that your membership fee for the coming year was wrongly quoted to you as £125. This did not take into consideration the fact that, as you have been a member for over 5 years, you are entitled to a 10% reduction in your membership fees. The correct price is therefore £112.50. We regret this mistake and hope it did not cause you too much inconvenience.

As you are aware, membership fees are due by the end of this month and we are enclosing a renewal form for you to complete. We should be grateful if you could ensure that we receive this no later than 31 March so that you can continue to use the facilities as before.

Complimentary close → Yours sincerely

Signature space

Name and designation →
Mark Pickup
Deputy Manager

Enclosure → Enc

The letterhead reads:

ACME FITNESS CLUB
Barchester Road
HIGHTOWN
HG2 9PL

Tel: 08171-598983
Fax: 08171-600300

E-mail: admin@acmefit.co.uk
Web site: www.acmefit.co.uk

A standard letter

Key items in a letter

The reference is usually the initials of the writer and the person who typed the letter. The file number may also be added, eg KM/LM/2030.

The date is normally written as date/month/year in a letter i.e. 21 June 2002.

The name and address of the recipient. The recipient is the person who will receive the letter. There is usually no punctuation in the address and the town is typed in CAPITALS. If possible, put the postcode on a separate line and *never* punctuate it.

Many organisations include the title of the person (Mr, Mrs, Miss, Dr) but some do not. Many women prefer the title 'Ms' and you can use this if you do not know whether a woman is married or not.

The salutation is the part that says 'Dear Mr Naru' or Dear Miss O'Hare'. The title used here must match that used in the address line. A formal letter may start Dear Sir or Dear Madam. A personal letter may start with just the first name, e.g. Dear Abbas or Dear Kate. *Never* write the first name *and* the surname or family name. Dear Fred is fine. Dear Mr Smith is fine. Dear Mr F Smith is wrong – and so is Dear Mr Fred Smith!

A heading is often included so that the recipient can quickly see what the letter is about. If you use capitals and/or bold then you don't need to underscore your heading.

The main part of the letter is divided into paragraphs. There may be just one paragraph in a simple letter and several in a complex one. Start each paragraph at the left hand margin, unless you are told to do something different. Leave a blank space between each one.

The complimentary close used today is normally either 'Yours faithfully' or 'Yours sincerely'. (Check that you can spell 'sincerely' properly!) The complimentary close should match the salutation:

Dear Sir or Dear Madam *use* Yours faithfully
Dear Mr Smith *use* Yours sincerely

A business letter starting Dear Fred may end with just the word Sincerely, or Best wishes or Yours truly or Kind regards. Type what the writer wants you to type – but note that the second word in a salutation *never* starts with a capital letter.

The signature space is necessary for the writer to sign the letter. Most people leave about 5 blank spaces but you should adjust this if the person who will sign the letter has very large or small handwriting.

The name and designation of the person signing the letter is shown below the signature. The designation is the person's official title in the organisation.

The enclosure abbreviation is added if any documents are being send with the letter. This is usually typed as Enc (for one document) or Encs (for more than one). This tells both the mailroom *and* the recipient to check there is something else in the envelope. It also reminds you to enclose it as well!

Rules to follow

There are some basic rules to follow when you are typing a business letter. The most important are listed below.

- It is not usual to include contracted words in a business letter, such as *can't, isn't, won't*. Instead you should type *cannot, is not* and *will not*.

- Abbreviated words are not used, such as *rep, phone* or *thru*, even though these may be handwritten. Instead you should convert these to the full version, e.g. *representative, telephone* or *through*.

- Slang expressions are not normally used but a rather more formal type of language is, e.g. '*We hope this is OK*' would be '*We hope this meets with your approval*'. The only exception would be if your line manager or team leader was writing to someone he or she knew very well.

Memos

The word memo is an abbreviated way of saying 'memorandum' ('memoranda' is the correct plural word).

A memo is an *internal* document – so there is no need to put the person's address. Other differences are described below.

- Memos have a simplified standard layout at the top, which usually includes the following items:

  TO – after which you type the name of the recipient and, sometimes, his or her designation

  FROM – after which you type the sender's name and, in some organisations, his or her designation

  DATE – usually typed in full, as in a letter

  REFERENCE – again normally the writer's initials and then the typist's.

  Do note that the order of these items can vary – so check your heading carefully so that you make sure you put each entry in the correct place.

  It is also better if you start to type each entry at the same point by using your Tab or Indent key.

- Sometimes you will see a printed heading for SUBJECT. In other cases you can just type the subject heading, if there is one, before the text, then leave a blank line.

- There is no salutation or complimentary close.

- Memos are never signed in full but are usually initialled by the sender.

```
                          MEMO

TO      Sinead Regan, Zeenat Khan      cc Helen O'Neill

FROM    Mark Pickup

DATE    17 March 2002

REF     MP/ML

MEMBERSHIP SUBSCRIPTIONS

We have now had a number of complaints and queries from members about their subscription
renewal. Those who have been members for over five years are entitled to a 10% reduction and
those who have been members for over three years are entitled to a 5% reduction. It appears that
these reductions have not been taken into account when the renewal forms have been issued.

To solve this problem can you please arrange for the following action to be taken as a matter of
urgency

1    Check the computer database of members and find out why this problem occurred.

2    Send a letter of apology to all members who have been affected with a new renewal notice.

3    Ensure that all staff are aware we are doing this, in case we receive any more telephone
     enquiries.

Ideally I would like all these letters to be sent before the end of this week, as renewal payments are
due on 31 March.

MP
```

A memo

- The 'style' of a memo is usually less formal than a business letter –
  but not always. If your boss was writing a memo to a senior
  manager about an important topic, it may be written in quite a
  formal tone.

- It is normal to send a memo on a particular subject or topic. This
  makes it easier to file. Some junior typists occasionally make the
  mistake of 'grouping' subjects under one memo when separate
  memos should have been sent. If you are in any doubt about this,
  check with the person who gave you the work to do.

- Memos are normally set out very clearly, so that they are easy to
  read. If there are several points to make, these may be listed as
  numbered points (or bullet points, like these paragraphs). This
  makes it easier to read important parts.

- You may be asked to send the same memo to several people. There
  are two ways of doing this.
  - If there are only a few people, it is normal to write all their
    names after the TO heading.

－ If there are so many that you couldn't fit them all in the space, type 'See below' and list everyone's name at the bottom under the heading 'Distribution'. Alphabetical order is often used, so that no-one can take offence about where their name is in the order!

It is a good idea, after you have typed and copied the memo, to tick off each person's name on their own copy. This helps you to check you haven't missed anyone.

● If you need to send a copy of a memo to someone, then type *cc* (for carbon copy) towards the end of the TO line and put their name. You may sometimes see *bcc*. This stands for blind carbon copy. This is only written on the copy of the person(s) receiving the blind copy. This is because the sender doesn't want other recipients to know about these copies.

● Today many organisations store a template of their memo paper on computer. This is much easier than trying to insert names against printed headings when you are using a computer. Otherwise, you can use plain paper and type in the headings yourself.

Check it out!

1　Check out the layout of memos where you work – or at your college. If possible, try to obtain different examples to see the differences.

2　Find out if anyone at work or in your group accesses a memo heading as a template on their computer system. If your office or your college operates Office 2000, you can see these yourself in your word processing package when you Open a New document.

3　Discuss with your tutor or supervisor why blind carbon copies may be sent and where the term 'carbon copy' originated.

E-mail messages

Although you will learn more about e-mail if you continue your studies to level 2, it is important you know about basic messages. This is because many companies now have e-mail throughout the organisation and in this case, even as a junior employee, you would have your own e-mail address and be able to send messages. This means you can use e-mail to pass on important information or urgent messages quickly without moving from your desk.

However, there are certain disadvantages. The first is that, if your written English is poor, this will be on view to everyone.

The second disadvantage is that simply sending an e-mail message does not guarantee the recipient has read it! However, on all internal systems you can check on your screen whether the mail you sent has been opened. If it has not, and the message was urgent or important, you still need to go and find someone and tell them.

The third disadvantage is that you may have no permanent record of what you have done if you delete the e-mail from your mailbox without taking a paper copy.

The style of e-mails

- E-mails are usually informal – but you must still watch your 'tone' if you are sending a message to a senior colleague!
- The computer will automatically put your name or ID and the date and time on the top of each message.
- If you are replying to a message, the name of the recipient will be entered automatically.
- You need to put an entry on the subject line, which summarises the reason for sending it.
- Keep the message short and simple. You can use your spelling checker to check spelling errors, although you will still need to check it yourself. Use paragraphs and punctuation *properly*.
- There is no 'rule' about whether to put your name at the bottom. It will be printed at the top, automatically, anyway. Whether you repeat it again is up to you.

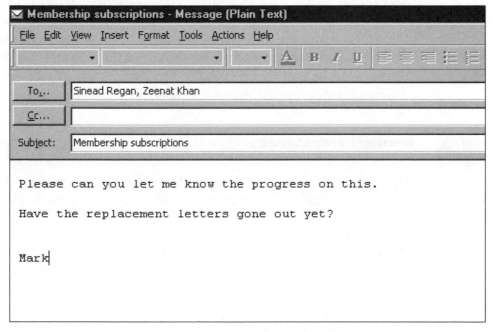

An e-mail

E-mail pitfalls

● Because e-mails are informal and easy to use, some people think that they can say what they want on e-mail – tell jokes, make personal remarks and so on. *Never* be tempted to do this. Not only could someone take offence or be upset, your employer has the legal right to monitor everything you send by e-mail. If you abuse your e-mail privilege, disciplinary action can be taken against you.

● Because e-mails can be sent quickly, it is tempting to write and send them without thinking or checking the content properly. If you are in doubt about sending any information by e-mail, ask your team leader or another team member for advice and *always* check, before you press 'send', that you are sending it to the correct person!

● Never type an e-mail in capital letters. This is called SHOUTING and is considered impolite.

Information update

In October 2000, a law was passed which allows senior managers to read any routine communication which is sent in their organisation without consent. This has strengthened the ability of employers to take action if they are suspicious about the content of e-mails sent by their staff.

It has always been against the law to send malicious and untrue gossip by e-mail – or in any other form. This is known as libel (or slander if it is spoken). Today many companies have an IT policy which states how staff must use computer facilities, such as e-mail and the Internet. Many have also 'tightened' up security on their e-mail facilities – so that staff cannot send or receive e-mails with inappropriate content (such as swear words). Under the new rules, staff guilty of wasting time by gossiping over e-mail, surfing holiday sites and accessing chat rooms on the Internet during work time are just as likely to be formally disciplined as those who try to download inappropriate material or conduct a romance over e-mail!

Check it out!

Find out your employer's or your college's IT policy. Write down how this affects you when you are sending e-mails or accessing the Internet.

Then investigate how the disciplinary policy works and what steps would be taken against anyone who was found sending an inappropriate e-mail. In some organisations, for instance, the penalty is instant dismissal.

Test your knowledge and understanding

1   Respond to these instructions from your team leader, Stephanie Walker whose official title is Sales Administrator.

'Can you do a short letter to Marianne Pickup, 15 Wetherby Road, Hightown, HG2 6MP, please. Date it today. Start it Dear Miss Pickup. Say: Thank you for your recent letter regarding the non-delivery of the coat you ordered from us at the end of last month. Then start a new paragraph. Unfortunately, the delay was caused by problems at our warehouse. These have now been resolved and the coat has been sent to you by special delivery. Final paragraph – We are sorry if this delay has caused you any inconvenience and thank you for shopping with us. Then end it appropriately.

2   Reread the memo which Mark Pickup sent shown on page 95. If you were Sinead or Zeenat, and the work was delayed because of a computer fault which has now been rectified, and the letters are being sent out later today, how would you word your reply to Mark? Draft a short, simple – but polite – memo in response.

Evidence collection

You need to start to collect examples of documents you have prepared as your evidence for this element. Ideally, you need to obtain:

- a copy of original documents you have received for typing (both handwritten and in typescript)
- notes of the questions you asked when you queried anything you didn't understand – and the answers you were given
- a copy of the draft document, before you made any corrections
- a copy of the final document, after any corrections or changes were made.

It is sensible to talk to your supervisor about this, as there may be certain documents you cannot copy because they contain sensitive information. However, sometimes you can use these if you take a copy with the sensitive information omitted or blanked out. Don't be tempted to put copies to one side without telling anyone! You will do better if people know that you need these for your award and give their approval.

The importance of checking for errors

Many people take a lot of care over producing a document, and then do not check it properly. There are several very good reasons for checking your work carefully.

1   People will consider you slapdash and careless if you regularly give them sloppy or inaccurate work. They will think you can't spell or type properly.

2   Time and again, you will be in the embarrassing position of having your faults pointed out and doing the work all over again.

3   Retyping and correcting documents takes time. Therefore you will get behind with your other work and may miss an important deadline if the document is urgent.

4   You will never be trusted to complete a document and send it out on your own.

5   If a document you complete *isn't* checked by someone else, there is the danger that an inaccurate document could be sent.
    –   If a customer receives it, this gives the impression that the whole organisation is poor and slapdash – and the customer may well take his business elsewhere in future.
    –   If the document is sent internally, then your lack of checking ability is on display to everyone.
    –   If the error is one which is not immediately obvious, such as the wrong date or an incorrect number, then you may cause people considerable inconvenience if they think this information is correct.

    It's always much easier – and safer – to do it right first time!

The delivery service is rather erotic ...

How to proof-read documents for errors

There are three skills you need to proof-read documents properly.

1 Correct as you go skills

It makes sense to correct typing errors as you go. If you are a touch typist you should be watching your copy as you type but should also glance across at your screen regularly. If you are a good typist you will 'sense' errors as soon as your fingers go wrong! Then quickly glance at your screen to check. But be careful – when you glance back – to start again at the correct place.

If you are using a modern word processing package, such as Word 2000, your spelling errors will be underlined in red. In addition, common errors (such as nwe for new) will be corrected automatically.

Remember you can correct in several ways.

- Your delete key removes characters to the right of the insertion point.

- Your backspace key removes characters to the left of the insertion point.

- You can insert text you have missed simply by moving the insertion point at the correct placc, and typing in the words you need to add. This is because your Insert feature is 'on' as the default.

- You can overtype text by pressing the Insert key (to turn off Insert) and then typing over the incorrect text. However, this is a dangerous correction method as:

  - you may continue too long, and overtype words you want to keep

  - you may forget to press Insert again (to turn it back on). If you do, the next time you try to add text you will overtype it instead.

2 Checking after completion

To do this properly you need to learn how to read your work properly on screen. If you really struggle with this, take *one* print-out (preferably on a draft setting) and check this instead. But do develop your screen reading skills – to save both time and paper.

- Start by checking the length of your document to see that you have included all the headings and paragraphs.

- Check the content of each paragraph to make sure your eye hasn't 'jumped' and missed a line. If so, and you are using Word, you will probably see the text underlined in green to show a grammatical error. This is because it won't make sense.

- Use your spell-checker. On Word, you simply click the ABC icon on your toolbar at the top. On WordPerfect the quick way is to press Control and F2 together. The checker will move through your text, stopping at every wrong word and offering an alternative. You have to decide whether to accept or reject the alternative. If you have any doubts, ask a colleague before you make a decision.

- Check all figures and proper names against the original – your spell checker can't help you here.

- Read through the document yourself *word by word* to check:
  - if there are any mistakes the spell checker has missed
  - if it makes sense.

3 Checking the printout

The finished document should look attractive and neat on the page. Sometimes, however, even if the text is perfect things can go wrong when you print out. For instance:

- The paper may have misfed so the text is crooked on the page or the ink is smudged.

- The margins may be wrong in relation to any fixed heading.

- The start may be too high in relation to the printed heading.

- You may find the last line or two of text (or even worse, the last word) has carried over to another page. It is obviously silly, on a letter, for the signature space to be on one page and the name and designation on another!

If any of these problems occur you need to make minor adjustments before you print out again.

- If you have a printer problem, take out the paper, fan it, check it is positioned correctly against the paper guides and take another test print. If you are using an ink jet printer, don't touch the paper for a few seconds until it is dry.

- If you have a margin problem, then alter these. Access your help facility or check with a colleague or tutor if you have never done this before.

- If you want to stop a document going onto two pages, you can check to see if there is a space you can remove which would 'pull back' the text. Otherwise, you can alter the font size. This is shown at the top of your screen. Most documents are produced in 12 point, but if you highlight the text and select 11 point, you may find the text now fits easily onto one page.

A final warning. You may be tempted to use correction fluid to correct a minor blemish or mistake on a print-out. If you do, remember there is a right and wrong way of using it as you will see in the chart below.

Never ... ✗	Instead ... ✓
• use correction fluid which is the consistency of treacle because it's old or you didn't screw the top on tightly	• shake the bottle well before you use it
• splash it on as if you were painting the side of a house	• dip the brush *lightly* into the bottle and wipe it *gently* on the side to remove the surface
• use it to correct major mistakes Basically it should be kept for very minor *written* mistakes or the odd, tiny dirty mark	• *gently* put a *small* amount on the letters you want to correct or mark you want to remove
• use white correction fluid on coloured paper	• put the document to one side until the fluid has completely dried
• use it on a final print-out which will be sent externally	• screw the top back on very tightly.
• try to make a correction before the correction fluid has completely dried.	

The do's and don'ts of using correction fluid

The limitations of spell checkers

Most people think spell checkers are wonderful – and so they are. However, they have serious limitations. This is because they accept any *real* word, regardless of whether it has been correctly used or not!

Test your knowledge and understanding

1   The following paragraph has 10 errors. Four of these would not be shown by a spell checker. Can you identify which 4 these are – and then correct *all* of them?

> People who want to send e-mail messages 'on the move' have traditionally had to use a laptop computor – or send an abbreveated text message on there mobile. No longer! A new devise is on its way from America and Canada called the BlackBerry. This is a tiny, handheld gaget which allows users to send reel emales. The price is expected to bee around £400 and predictions are that this will be a far more poppular choice than laptops and mobile phones phones in the near future.

2   Using your common sense is another useful method of checking. Can you identify *all* the mistakes in following sentences, using your common sense, and then correct them?

   a   Mr Evans is traveling to France on Friday. He is staying at the Europa Hotel, Berlin.

   b   The meeting willstart at 2 am in room F235.

   c   Interest rates have been falling for the passed few years. This has meant people recieve more if they have a savings account.

   d   We can allow you a reduction of 15% on the list price of £250. Can you please, therefore, send us your check for £ 210.

3   On the next page is a document your team leader wants you to type. You found it in your 'in-tray' this morning marked urgent. Your team leader is currently at a meeting and not due back for an hour.

   a   Check through and note anything you cannot understand.

   b   Why should you try to find the answer to any queries as soon as possible?

   c   How would you do this in the team leader's absence?

   d   If possible, type up a clean copy of the document to prove you have understood it properly. See if you can find the two mistakes which have *not* been spotted by your team leader – and correct them!

BOLD
pse → IN-HOUSE TRAINING COURSES

All in-house training courses are held in the new training suite which comprises classrooms, seminar rooms, IT facilities with Internet access and research facilities. *[handwritten: centre, rooms]*

A wide variety of training courses are offered by the company.

Over the next few weeks, the following courses are being offered on on a first come, first served basis:

Date	Title
Monday, 6 April	Stress management
Wed, 8 April	Time managment
Friday, 10 April	Introduction to Powerpoint
(Poss Mon 13/4??)	Health and safety training
Tuesday, 14 April	Introduction to the company database
Thrusday, 16 April	customer service
Tuesday, 21 April	finding information on the Internet
Thursday, 23 April	Managing staff
Tuesday, 28 April	Introduction to spreadsheeets
Friday, 31 April	Basic first Aid

[handwritten annotations: in full; Need to check this; trs; uc; uc; lc]

If you are interestted, please see our line manager to obtain his/her approvel.

Then complete form T60, ask your line manager to sign it and send it to the staff traiing dept. *[handwritten: in full.]*

Jackie Kent
Training Manager
30.03.02

Using dictionaries to check for spelling

There are two types of words you will meet in business correspondence which may cause you problems: technical words or 'jargon' and ordinary words you've never met before.

Technical words, jargon and unknown words

Technical words vary from one industry to another. In the introduction to this book, you saw several words which relate to NVQs – such as 'assessor', 'verifier', 'evidence'. These are all NVQ 'jargon'. If you worked in a computer firm you would hear terms such as 'memory', 'code' and 'bytes' whereas a solicitor would talk about 'defendants', 'litigation' and 'executors'.

In any organisation, the jargon will seem very strange when you first start work. Sometimes it will include abbreviations as well as full words. The point with any unknown words is to:

- ask when you are not sure
- *never* guess a word or abbreviation
- remember what you are told.

Electronic dictionaries

Most word processing packages have a thesaurus or dictionary which will give you the meaning of a word you have typed. Some are better than others and provide clearer definitions. However, if you have a thesaurus, you will also see a list of alternative words – which is often useful to help you understand better what the word means. Dictionaries on CD are also available – as well as on-line. However, most people find it quicker and easier to look in a standard dictionary to find what they need.

Manual dictionaries

A good dictionary is invaluable. You will find information on:

- the part of speech of a word, e.g. whether it is a noun or a verb. This is important, because you may see the same word but it will have an entirely different meaning. Obvious examples are:

  a desert   to desert (someone)
  a ring   to ring
  a wave   to wave
- advice on spelling and the spelling variations that are allowed
- guidance on how words should be used
- hints on pronunciation.

To use a dictionary quickly, focus on the top right-hand corner of the page, which always gives the final word on that page. Use this to find the first letter of your word and a word near to yours in spelling. Then look at the tops of other columns, which again have the final word highlighted. Once you have found the column you want, you can look down to find the word you need.

The biggest problem is if you have no idea at all how to spell the word. If you are totally stuck, ask a colleague for help or access a thesaurus and see if you can find it by looking at groups of words which you think mean something similar.

Test your knowledge and understanding

1   Learn how to use the electronic dictionary in your word processing package. Check if you have a thesaurus and see if you can use that too. Then find out the difference between each of the following pairs of words.

    a   dissent   descent
    b   confident   confidant
    c   formerly   formally
    d   stationery   stationary

2   Use a manual dictionary to check each of the following pairs.

    a   proceed   precede
    b   lose   loose
    c   accept   except
    d   illegible   ineligible

3   Find out which descriptions you would like and which you would not by looking up the meanings of each of the following words.

    Identify whether you would be delighted or horrified if you heard yourself described as:

    a   charismatic
    b   always vacillating
    c   being parsimonious
    d   maligning your colleagues
    e   being obdurate
    f   often intransigent
    g   usually acquiescent

The importance of storing documents safely

Once all the checks have been made and the document has been approved, you need to:

- take any required copies
- distribute the document as requested
- make sure the person who gave you the work receives a copy – and their original is returned. In many offices, you will be asked to store these documents safely.

It is important that both the document and the original is safely stored. This is because:

- the document may be needed for reference at any time
- you may need either, or both, to answer any queries
- the person who gave you the work may want to refer to either document at a later date.

In addition, of course, you will also have an electronic copy if you prepared the document on computer. If you work for several people, it is sensible to set up different folders on your computer and to save each person's work in their own folder. Your supervisor or IT tutor will show you how to do this.

Give each document a clearly recognisable name. If you access the folder, you should then be able to spot the document quickly. Another simple trick is to note the date you typed it, if this is not printed on the hard copy. Then you can always search the folder using your Find facility, and enter the date. Your computer will then find all the documents you prepared on that date.

Evidence collection

1   You need to prove that you can use both the following types of checking methods:

   a   using a dictionary (either manual or electronic)

   b   asking your line manager.

   Your assessor may ask you to demonstrate how you use a dictionary. However, you can also prove this if you highlight words in a document you did not understand or know how to spell, and then write below the correct spelling and meaning. Include, too, the final print-out with the corrections.

   You will prove you ask your line manager if you produce documents for him and her and already have a record of the queries you have made and the answers you received. You can also ask your line manager for witness testimony to confirm that you always check when you are uncertain of anything you have to type.

2   Be prepared to explain to your assessor the methods you use to ensure you have kept the original and stored the document safely. Or you can write a brief account to explain this.

3   Finally, if you have had any problems producing a document on time for any reason, state:

   a   why the problem occurred

   b   who you told

   c   when you told them.

   Again, you could ask that person for witness testimony to say that you notified them in good time for alternative arrangements to be made.

Photocopy routine documents

Photocopying is a routine activity in most organisations. A variety of documents may need to be copied in several different ways. Everyone who works in an office needs to be able to do this type of job quickly and efficiently.

Using a photocopier correctly

There are literally hundreds of photocopiers on the market, ranging from very small machines to very large ones. In addition, there are a variety of different features.

- Some will only print black and white copies, others will reproduce colour originals.
- Some will just print copies, others will collate as well. Collating means putting the pages in a multi-page document in the correct order.
- Many will staple, in a variety of different places.
- Virtually all will enlarge or reduce text and graphics.
- Most will print out on either A4 or A3 paper – or on special mailing labels.
- Some will only scan hard (paper) copies whilst others can receive copying instructions direct from a computer..

First of all you need to find out the features on the photocopier *you* will be using. These will be described in great detail in the manual which arrives with the machine. There is often also a shortened version of this with the main instructions for operators. These can then be copied on the machine and placed in a user's manual nearby or put on the wall for users to read and check.

Photocopiers come in many different sizes

The key features of a photocopier

The main items you need to know and understand are listed below.

- **The exposure glass**. Originals can be placed on the glass print side down for copying. Look for indicators around the side which tell you where to position different sizes of paper, such as A4 or A5.

- **The document feeder**. Multi-page originals are placed here in a stack. The machine will automatically feed each one through in turn.

- **The paper tray(s)**. You may have one or more paper trays which hold photocopying paper.

- **The bypass tray**. This is used for photocopying onto special paper, such as card, labels or transparencies for overhead projectors.

- **The output tray**. This is where the photocopies emerge.

- **The power or on/off switch**. Photocopiers are normally left switched on all day. Some go into automatic 'sleep mode' overnight and start to warm up when someone approaches them in the morning! However, if you have a more basic machine, you need to know where the power switch is so that you can switch it on at the start of the day and off again at the end, *if* this is your job.

- **The control panel**. This will vary, depending upon your machine, but you can expect to see:

  - **number keys** for entering the number of copies you want
  - a **start key** to start copying
  - an **interrupt key** if you want to do a quick job in the middle of a longer one
  - **stop/clear key** to cancel an entry you have made or to stop photocopying if you have a problem
  - **special keys** or a **display panel** for entering instructions such as enlarge/reduce/collate/staple and for displaying error messages.

Parts of a photocopier

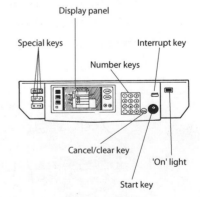

A photocopier control panel

Safety first!

It is important to know the specific hazards which relate to photocopiers and how to minimise any risks when using them.

Photocopiers: health and safety requirements

- All photocopiers must be positioned so they have a flow of air around them, be placed on a stable surface and away from humidity and dust. *Never* attempt to move any photocopier yourself.

- Never use an extension lead or adaptor – the plug must be put directly into a wall socket.

- *Immediately* turn off the power and disconnect the copier if:
  - you spill anything into the machine
  - the machine needs to be serviced or repaired (most machines signal this on the display panel)
  - the cover is broken or damaged.

- Dispose of used toner containers according to instructions. *Never* incinerate them or discard them near an open flame. Wash any spilled toner powder off your hands or clothes with cold water. Store toner containers in a cool, dry place, out of direct sunlight and on a flat surface. Note that used toner must never be used again. It must be disposed of.

- Keep paper clips, staples and other metallic objects well away from the machine, so they can't fall inside it. Most machines have a little tray for such items.

- Use only the recommended type of paper and fill the paper tray(s) according to the manual. Never use any type of metallic paper, paper with perforated lines or carbon paper.

- Clean the machine and the glass with a soft damp cloth, then wipe it with a dry cloth to remove any wet areas. Never use any chemical cleaners.

- Don't make copies with the lid open and stare at the light. Although the ultraviolet light will not actively harm your eyes, it won't do them any good either!

- Never try to remedy a fault unless you have been trained to do so. If you have been trained to remedy simple faults, never touch parts labelled with a warning or marked 'hot surface', otherwise you are likely to burn yourself.

- Check your own manual for other specific safety recommendations for your own machine.

Check it out!

1 Check through the table above and talk to your tutor or supervisor about any entry you do not fully understand.

2 Look at the manufacturer's instructions for using your own machine safely. Note any entries which are different from those in the table.

3 For the photocopier you are using, make sure you know where each of the items in the list of key features is situated.

Single page and multi-page copies

Sometimes you will copy a single page. On other occasions a document may consist of several pages.

Single originals

On many machines you can choose whether to place a single copy on the exposure glass or place it in the document feeder. Do make sure you have the print facing the right way (up or down), otherwise the result will be a blank page! You will always place an original print side down on the glass, but this may be different if you use the document feeder.

A flimsy original or very special document is always better placed on the glass to reduce the risk of damage. If you are copying a page from a book then you obviously must put this on the glass. Then close the lid. (It doesn't matter if this won't close properly, because of the thickness of the original.) You will not only obtain a better copy but will also protect your eyes from the bright ultraviolet light when the copy is made.

Multi-page originals

These will always be placed into the document feeder. *Always* make sure of the following.

- Check your original has no paperclips or staples in it. These need removing otherwise your document will jam.
- Check your original is in the correct order. Check it through *at least* twice! This is easier if your document has numbered pages. If you fail to do this, your copies will also be in the wrong order and will need resorting.
- Do check if any pages in your original have print on both sides. If you simply stack the document into the feeder only one side will be copied. You must then copy the other side of any two-sided pages and insert these at the correct place.

Single copies face down on the glass

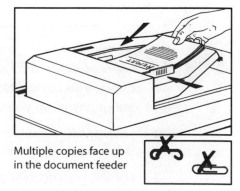

Multiple copies face up in the document feeder

Making single or multiple copies

Single copies

You will normally select the number of copies you need on a key pad. The 'default' is one copy. This means that if you don't key in any other number you will obtain a single copy. Remember that if you make a mistake, you can press Cancel and do it again.

Multiple copies

Frequently you will be asked to make several copies of a document. If the document is also a multi-page one, you have to take care not to waste paper. It is simple to re-print one copy of a single page which is poor quality. It is a different matter if you have just taken 20 copies of a 15-page document and they are all useless!

You will have no problems if you do this operation in stages:

- check a multi-page document is in the right order
- take *one* **sample copy** and check the quality (see below)
- if the quality is good, carefully key in the number of copies you want (minus one, because you have just made one!)
- replace the document in the document feeder
- press the Start key
- stay near the machine in case there are any problems, such as running out of paper
- collect your copies from the output tray.

Checking quality

A quality photocopy is one which is immediately usable and which doesn't need 'explaining' away to your boss because something went wrong! This means:

- the paper is smooth and not crumpled or torn
- the image (i.e. printed part) is perfectly clear
- the image is positioned in the correct place on the paper
- all the pages have been copied
- you have taken the right number of copies
- all the pages in a multipage document are in the right order
- you have remembered to return the original.

Paper can become crumpled if you experience a misfeed. Until you have been trained to do this, you need to notify someone who can remedy the problem. You then need to take another copy to replace the spoiled one.

You will have no problems with the image if:

- you *always* take a **sample copy**
- you check this carefully
- you learn how to make minor adjustments if the image is too dark or too light
- you know exactly how to reposition the image if it is in the wrong place.

You will have no problems doing the job correctly if:

- you have noted down what was required
- you have worked methodically and according to instructions
- you have cleared up after yourself and not left anything behind (such as the original on the glass!).

Check it out!

1   Sample copies are so useful that many photocopiers now have this facility. You simply press the 'sample copy' key to take a test copy. Find out if your machine has such a key.

2   Very dark or light print can cause problems, so can coloured paper or coloured print. If possible, take photocopies of documents with poor print quality, on coloured paper and with coloured print and learn how to make the adjustments on your copier to improve the quality.

Information update

Do be careful what you copy! Copyright law means that you cannot just copy anything you want – such as a magazine, newspaper or book – without permission. In certain circumstances, copying for personal use is allowed, for instance, if you are a student. Your college or local library will have the details, or ask your supervisor.

Minimising wastage

Near every photocopier you are likely to find a large rubbish bin. Try not to use it! Not only is it costly and wasteful of paper but it also wastes your time if you have to do a job all over again.

You can minimise wastage by always remembering to do the following.

- Check your original(s) before you start. Repair any torn pages. Remove any dirty marks with *special* photocopier correction fluid. Wait until it is *completely* dry before putting the document on the exposure glass.
- Check the exposure glass is clean. If there are any marks on it (or blobs of correction fluid!) these will come out as black marks on your copy. If the glass is dirty, wipe it with a *damp* (not wet) cloth.
- Never be tempted to use paper which isn't meant for the job. If you refill the paper tray, always use the right paper.
- Place the original correctly and *always* take a sample copy. Check this carefully before you make any more.
- Always check you have keyed in the number correctly before you press Start and never take extra copies 'just in case'.
- Learn how to stop printing quickly if something is wrong.

Finally, in many organisations people are encouraged to make double-sided copies of routine or internal multi-page documents. This saves paper because the paper is copied on both sides. You may hear this called **duplexing**.

How to do this will vary depending upon your machine. If you have a very basic machine it is impossible – and if you have a very sophisticated machine it may be quite complicated. However, it is a useful skill to learn.

The importance of sorting and fastening documents correctly

Two operations which are often linked to multipage photocopying are:

- sorting or **collating** the pages (this means putting them in the correct order)
- fastening the pages – usually by **stapling.**

Some machines will do both operations for you. Others will only do one and some will do neither! You therefore need to know how to sort and fasten both manually and on the machine.

Collating a document

A collator is simply a set of small trays stacked one on top of the other (see illustration). If your machine collates, you will often see these at one side of your machine. If you select 'collate' then the machine will put the first page face down in each tray, then the second and so on. So you can simply lift the completed sets out of all the trays. The number of trays used obviously depends upon the number of copies. If you need to do more copies than you have trays, then you have to do the job over and over until it is completed. An alternative, with some machines, is that the collated sets are off-set in one tray, so you can easily separate them. The critical point is not to drop the papers on the floor at any time!

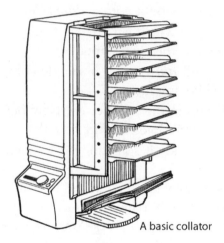

A basic collator

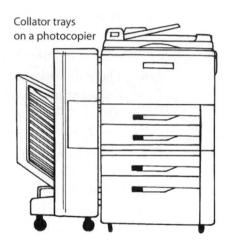

Collator trays on a photocopier

Collator trays are very useful

If you have no collator, then you must do this task yourself. This is where working carefully, neatly and methodically really pays off. You need a large surface. As you obtain copies of page one, turn these face down, and spread them out, on the working surface. Then add page two, then page three and so on. You should know if you've gone wrong (e.g. by putting two of page 3 on one pile) because you will be short of a page before you have completed all the sets.

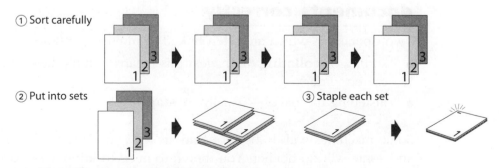

① Sort carefully

② Put into sets

③ Staple each set

Manual collating requires careful methodical working

You need to do a final check that all your sets are complete and all the pages are in the right order. Collating many copies of a very large document by hand can be very tedious. This is one job where team work is invaluable if you can find someone who will help you.

Fastening photocopies

You may be asked to use a paperclip to fasten the pages together, but more often you will be asked to staple them. If your machine can staple automatically, you can select the position of the staple, or the number to be used. The most usual options are the top left (at an angle, if you prefer) or down the left hand side.

If you are stapling yourself, then use the stapler *safely* and staple the pages *sensibly*. Remember that the print must *never* be obscured at any point.

- Put the stapler on a flat, clear surface.
- If the document has very many pages you will have to use a heavy duty stapler. An ordinary one won't work.
- If you are stapling in the top left corner, place the staple just over a centimetre from the corner. Never put it so low that you staple over the text on *any* page.
- Don't angle the staple if this makes it difficult for you, line it up with the top or side edge of the paper.
- Keep your fingers out of the way!
- Learn how to unjam a stapler *safely* – and how to refill it. Always unplug an electric stapler before you do either of these operations.

Test your knowledge and understanding

Now check whether you can remember all the terms and important points in this element. Do this by deciding whether each statement below is True or False. Then check your answers with those given on page 227.

1 All photocopiers are the same.
2 All photocopiers need a good air flow all around them.
3 A flimsy or important original should be placed in the document feeder.
4 Dirty exposure glass will result in dirty and spoiled copies.
5 It is sensible to always take a couple of extra copies 'just in case'.
6 Stapling is so easy nothing can ever go wrong.
7 You should switch off the photocopier as soon as you have finished using it.
8 You can 'clean up' a dirty original by using special correction fluid.
9 You should always take a sample copy first, and check it carefully, before doing any more.
10 Another word for 'sorting' multipage copies is 'collating'.

Evidence collection

You need to prove that you can produce the number of photocopies you are asked to, that you always check the quality is acceptable, that you do all you can to waste as little paper as possible and that you can sort and fasten copies securely and in the right order.

Start a collection of photocopies you make. On this occasion you can do one more than you would normally need! Ideally some should be single page and some should be multiple pages. For each example, complete the form below. To help you, a blank form is included on page 239 which you can photocopy!

Photocopier record

Your name ....

No of originals:	No of copies required:	Other requirements (eg sorting and fastening copies)

Quality checks you made:

Methods you used to minimise waste paper:

Work undertaken satisfactorily .... Date
....
(This should be signed by the person who requested the work)

Photocopier problems you can correct yourself

Photocopiers are like many other pieces of equipment. They go wrong – often at the worst possible time, such as when you are in a hurry or have an important job to do. It is then that you may rush the job and cause a few problems for yourself!

The two problems you must know how to deal with yourself are these.

- The photocopier runs out of paper. In this case no more prints will emerge and there will normally be a warning that you are out of paper on the screen.
- You position the original wrongly. In this case you will have a poor quality copy as proof!

Replenishing the paper

There is normally a spare supply of paper kept near the photocopier and the main paper store is kept locked in a stationery cupboard.

Photocopier paper needs to be stored carefully, so it is kept wrapped, stored flat and kept in a dry place. Otherwise it jams in the machine. You also need to use the right type of paper for your machine – so always check you know which type to use if you have several in your stockroom or cupboard.

You need to know the following.

- How to open the paper tray. This may slide out or there may be a cover you open.
- How much paper it holds when full. There is normally a limit mark which shows the maximum it will hold. You must never put paper above this mark.

The steps to follow are as follows.

- Learn the knack of opening a box of photocopying paper! These are fastened with a plastic strap. You can either cut it with scissors *or* lie the box on its side and where the strap meets underneath, separate the ends by pulling the bottom strap first.
- Put the box the right way up and remove one packet of paper.
- Take the paper out of the packet.
- 'Square' the paper. This means making sure it is straight vertically and horizontally. The easiest way to do this is to hold it firmly at each side and give it a sharp tap, two or three times, on a firm surface.
- Place the paper in the tray against the guides. There is often an illustration in or by the tray to show you how to do this.
- Close the paper tray.

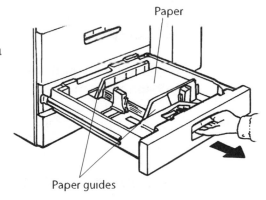

Paper

Paper guides

Refilling the paper tray

Repositioning the original

The most difficult originals to position are those with very narrow margins or which are on a small piece of paper (e.g. A5) and you want the print-out to be central on A4 paper. Newer machines will accept A5 originals quite easily but some older ones take the huff – and tell you that you need A5 paper in the paper tray! You need to find out how to cope with this on your machine. On some you can press Start again to over-ride this. If not, put a blank sheet of A4 behind your smaller original to fool the machine!

In the first case you may 'cut off' some of the print by accident. In the second you may struggle to put the original in the right position.

Sometimes you have to experiment to find the best place. If you take a sample copy each time then you will waste as little paper as possible. It may help to remember that positioning a document is like looking in a mirror – you have to do the opposite of what you think you need to do to get the required result! So if you want more blank space on the right, you may have to move the document to the left! Experience will help here.

Other types of problems

Problems can occur because of routine housekeeping and maintenance requirements and because of faults. On modern machines, these will be indicated by a symbol on the panel. Sometimes the machine can still be used, sometimes not.

The first thing you need to know is *who* to contact if you experience a problem you can't deal with yourself. The second is to remember that, no matter how tempted you may be, you should *never* try to rectify any type of fault unless you have been trained to do so.

The table on the next page summarises the type of problems and faults which may occur when you are using the machine – and the action you should take.

Note: If a *serious* problem occurs when you are on your own then switch off the machine and disconnect it from the electricity supply. You should do this if, for instance, you smell burning. Then obtain assistance quickly.

Finally, if you have a machine-related problem, then this may mean that you cannot complete the work you have to do on time. It is then important that you report the matter to the relevant person promptly so that alternative action can be taken – such as finding another machine which can be used.

Problem	What has happened	Action to take
Paper jam	There is a misfeed in the paper travelling from the paper tray through the machine.	Copying will have stopped. Notify the person in charge of rectifying paper jam. Do not attempt to clear this yourself.
Toner low	The toner (powdered ink) is running out.	You can continue to do a small job but should notify the person who can replenish the toner. Copies will become very faint unless this is done.
No staples	The staples have run out or have jammed.	You can continue to copy but cannot do automatic stapling until the stapler cartridge has been refilled or cleared. Notify the person who can do this.
Unknown error message	Something else has gone wrong and your machine is trying to tell you what it is!	Stop copying and notify the person responsible for the machine or your supervisor.

Evidence collection

1   Keep a log or record of any types of problems you encounter. You must be able to prove that you can:

  - cope yourself if the photocopier runs out of paper
  - make the proper adjustments if an original is wrongly positioned.

  If these happen as you are working then your supervisor or tutor can watch you and give you witness testimony. If not, you will have to show your assessor what you would do in this situation.

2   If any other problems occur which you must report to someone else, then write a short account of what happened and what you did. Ask the person to whom you reported the problem to countersign your account to prove it is true. If no problems occur when you are photocopying you are very lucky! However, do expect your assessor to ask what type of problems *may* occur and ask if you know who you would report them to.

3   Finally, if a problem – or anything else occurs – which means you cannot complete work on time, again say what you did and who you told. Ask that person to sign your statement to agree it is true.

Unit 104 — Find and store files in a paper-based system

> This unit is one of two Optional Group A units. You need to do *either* this unit *or* unit 105 to gain your award, but not both.

This unit is concerned with how you:

- find files when you are using a paper-based filing system
- update and store files in this type of system.

It is **important** because:

- every business organisation creates and receives many documents every day
- many of these documents are kept for future reference
- documents often need to be found quickly
- all documents *must* be stored safely and in the right place.

There are two elements to this unit. First, you need to understand all the main points relating to the paper-based filing systems which operate in all organisations.

Key skills signpost

If you are taking your Key Skills award in Problem Solving at level 1, then you can develop your knowledge of paper-based filing and use this as evidence for your Key Skills portfolio.

You have two problems to solve in relation to filing. These are described below.

1   Your customer files have increased rapidly over the past few months. You have an alphabetical system and some popular files are now very congested so it is difficult to fit new letters into it any more. Yesterday, a folder ripped when you were getting it out because it was jammed in so tightly.

2   Although you have a proper system for borrowing files, this only works when you are at your desk! When you are away, people seem to help themselves to files so you don't know where you are. It is difficult to say very much because most of the staff are older or more senior than you. Your problem comes when you are asked for a file which is missing and you don't know where to find it.

Alternatively, your supervisor or tutor may wish to help you identify a different problem relating to filing in a paper-based system which you could tackle.

PS1.1　Arrange a meeting with your supervisor or tutor at which you agree the problem and decide the best way to go about tackling it.

After the meeting, write a description of the problem yourself. Then suggest at least *two* ways in which it could be solved. Then consider which of your ideas are likely to be the most successful.

PS1.2　Arrange another meeting with your supervisor or tutor at which you can discuss your suggestions.

Decide how you will try out your plan and what you will do next. Write a short account of what was agreed and the steps you must now take to try to solve *both* problems.

Carry out your plan and make notes about the result.

PS1.3　Check if the problem has now been solved.

Write a short account of the results of your actions.

Explain what you have learned from this which would help you to improve your approach to problem solving in the future.

Find and store files in a paper-based system

Every organisation needs a good filing system so that *all* types of documents which are received and created can be:

- stored easily
- kept safely
- found quickly.

Using the filing system

Most filing systems are designed to be used by several people. However, all these users must know what they are doing. Even one piece of paper filed in the wrong place can cause problems for everyone because it can't be found quickly or easily!

Before you use any filing system, therefore, you will be trained how to use it. However, remember that your organisation may have slightly different systems from those described here. Secondly, there may be some files which cannot be accessed by everyone because they contain confidential information – for example, personal information about members of staff.

For that reason, it is important that you have specific permission from your team leader, supervisor or line manager before you use the system.

The importance of effective filing systems

A filing system is effective if:

- all the different types of documents can be stored easily
- all the documents are kept safely and in good condition
- the filing system is neat and tidy so it is easy to use
- people regularly and quickly find what they want.

An effective filing system is neat and tidy

The number and type of documents

Documents may range from single pieces of paper to booklets or catalogues. Some may be copies of letters or invoices which have been sent out, some will be correspondence which has been received. Others may be particularly important – such as a legal contract; they may be very large – such as plans for a new building, or very small – such as copy receipts. Remember that an effective filing system must be able to cope with all these different types of documents.

The consequences of a poor system

The first consequence of a lost document is an increase in stress as everyone tries to find it. The second is an increase in wasted time because the staff who are looking for the document should be doing other work.

If it still cannot be found then, at the very least, there will be a delay whilst another copy is obtained. With a very important document, however, this may not be possible – or may take a considerable time. Meanwhile, work will be delayed or people will be trying to work without the most up-to-date information.

In this situation, your organisation could be in danger of losing an order or losing a customer.

The requirements of an effective system

For a system to be effective there must be:

- specialist filing equipment
- the correct filing stationery and accessories
- proper training for all users

Filing equipment

When you start work you will find files stored in a number of different ways. The main variations are listed below.

- **Vertical filing** is the most common. Files are stored in large drawers in a cabinet. Two, three, four and five drawer cabinets are available but the most common are four drawer.
- **Lateral filing** relates to files which are placed side by side in a cabinet. Some cabinets are designed to be multi-purpose, with files at the top and shelves for other supplies lower down.
- **Horizontal filing** is when documents are placed in small drawers in a cabinet. These are useful for documents which are very large or must not be hole punched, such as drawings and photographs.
- **Rotary filing** is similar to the system you see in some shops where books or postcards rotate on a stand. You can simply turn the stand to find the file you want.

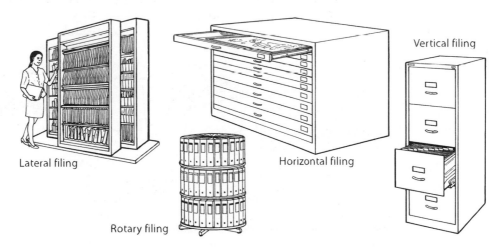

File can be stored in a number of ways

Filing stationery

Within any system the documents must be grouped and labelled so that they are easy to find.

- **File folders** are available in which documents are placed. They are normally fastened in the folder for security. The folder may be plain brown (the cheapest) or a variety of different colours. Coloured folders are easier to find, and some systems include 'colour coding' to help you find certain types of files more easily. Some file folders have a 'tab' at the top on which you can write the name of the file.

- **Document** (or **envelope**) **wallets** are often used to store papers on a temporary basis, especially if the file may be frequently borrowed to be carried out or taken to meetings.

- **Suspension files** are 'pockets' which hold files. These hang down inside a cabinet drawer or along a lateral cabinet. The best type are those which are linked together at the top as this prevents a folder 'disappearing' between two pockets. It would fall to the floor in a cupboard, but if you were operating in a cabinet drawer, you might never find the folder again! Pockets are designed so a label can be attached. Some have a clear plastic fastening in which you slide the name of the file. On others you 'clip' the plastic fastening on after inserting the name.

- **Lever arch files and box files** are two of the other types of filing accessories available. Lever arch files are like a very large ring binder and are used for specific documents which can be hole punched. Box files are the same size but are used for brochures and booklets which cannot (or must not) be punched.

- **Other accessories** are required if you are going to do the job properly. You need a method of fastening the documents into a folder. Both metal clips and laces are available. You also need to punch the documents accurately. It is better to use a proper heavy duty punch with a guide ruler.

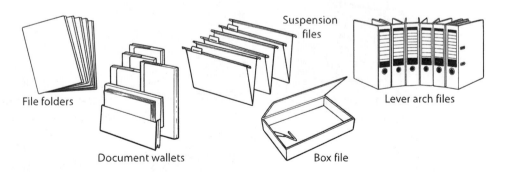

Different types of folders and files are available

Check it out!

Look through a stationery catalogue and identify all the different types of equipment and materials illustrated above. List the items you would choose if you were setting up a simple filing system to keep all your personal documents safely at home.

Alphabetical and numerical filing systems

There are two main filing systems in operation in most organisations. You need to know how to use both of them.

Alphabetical filing systems

These are the easiest systems to use, because you are simply following the letters of the alphabet.

- In most alphabetical systems the files will be stored by **name** – either the name of the customer or the name of the organisation.
- In other alphabetical systems the files may be stored by **subject**.
- In others, the files are stored by **geographical area**.

Alphabetical filing by name

The *Phone Book* is an excellent example of alphabetical filing by name. A good way of testing that you can quickly *find* a name alphabetically is to look up several names in the *Phone Book*.

In a filing system, you have to find files by knowing the order in which the names would appear. To do this quickly, you need to understand the rules you must follow.

Names of individuals	Names of organisations
The surname is always first	Ignore the word The, e.g. Happy Cattery, The
Short surnames are placed before long ones, e.g. Brow, Brown, Browne	Change numbers to words, e.g. Four Hills Hospital
If the surnames are the same, refer to the first name or initial, e.g. Brown G, Brown L	If the name is identical, follow street or town, e.g. Four Hills Hospital, Crewe; Four Hills Hospital, Croydon.
Initials are placed before full names, e.g. Brown L, Brown Lee	Put initials before names, e.g. BM Software, Backup Software
Names starting with Mac or Mc are all treated as 'Mac' and *normally* come before 'M', e.g. MacIntosh, McWhirter, Masters	Saint and St are all treated as 'Saint', e.g. Saint Augustine's Church, St John's School
Ignore any apostrophes, e.g. O'Neil is ONeil.	A public body, such as the local council, is filed under the name or town, e.g. Bath City Council, Benefits Agency.
Ignore d' and de' – so 'de Havilland' would be filed under 'H'	

Alphabet filing rules

Test your knowledge and understanding

Follow the filing rules to decide the order in which the following files would be placed in a cabinet. Remember to reverse the names of people so that the surname is always first.

Robert Fairbrother	Ken P Osborne	Option Technology
Belmont District Council	Waverley County Council	Gordon McMahon
Saleem and Co	PWS Packaging	Panorama Sport
Majid K A	A J Watson	St Ives Media Company
Equinox Motors	One Stop Copy Shop	MS Car Sales
EOM Publishing	Pat O'Reilly	The Farmers Arms

Alphabetical filing by topic

Sometimes you will find files ordered by topic, or subject, rather than by name. Your line manager (or tutor) may keep files like this because all the documents which relate to a particular topic are kept in one place.

When a topic is very large, it may be sub-divided into different areas. Both the topics themselves *and* any sub-divisions are put into strict alphabetical order, for instance:

Advertising		
Computer equipment		
Conferences		
Exhibitions		
Publicity	–	displays
	–	exhibitions
Staff	–	appointments
	–	records
	–	references

Alphabetical filing by place

An organisation which had customers all over the world may start by dividing its files geographically. Within each country, customers would then be filed alphabetically. In the UK, sales territories may be divided up geographically and customers filed in each area.

Again both the main area (country or county) and then the customers are *all* sorted into strict alphabetical order, e.g.:

Australia	–	Kookamere Carpets pty
		Sydney Fabrics
Canada	–	Interexperience Inc
		Toronto Tufting
		Vancouver Associates
France	–	Lefebre et Cie

Test your knowledge and understanding

You have started work for John Robbins, Sales Manager of Acme Furniture. John has two types of filing systems he wants you to understand.

- Information on products made by the company is stored under topic order.
- Furniture shop branch files are stored geographically by county and then by town.

For each of the lists below, put them into the order you would find them in John's filing system. Remember you need to put *both* the main topic *and* the sub-divisions into alphabetical order.

1   Tables – dining, coffee, occasional
    Cabinets – bedside
    Beds – single, double, king-size
    Desks – children's, office
    Chairs – lounge, dining.

2   Kent – Canterbury, Ashford, Sevenoaks, Maidstone
    Cornwall – Penzance, Falmouth, Truro, Newquay
    Cheshire – Nantwich, Crewe, Chester, Altrincham
    Yorkshire – Leeds, Bradford, Sheffield, Halifax

Numerical filing systems

There are two types of numerical filing systems you need to understand.

- The first relates to files stored in **number order.**
- The second relates to files stored in **chronological** – or **date – order**. This occurs when the date is the most important item on a document.

Filing by number

In this case, each file has its own number. This system is often used by large organisations as it is easier to keep adding additional files – you just allocate the next number. This is easier because all new files are added at the end – and not in the middle of popular letters, such as B or R.

To find a file which has been stored by its number, you obviously have to know what number it is – so a separate **index** is necessary. How to use an index is covered on page 131.

The danger with a numerical system is that you misread or 'transpose' the number by turning it round. Or if your writing isn't clear people can't tell whether you have written a 3, a 5 or an 8!

Filing by date

Within a file folder *all* documents should be fastened by date – with the most recent document on top. This makes sense because it is usually the most recent document that people want to read. They don't want to have to wade through six months of paper to find it!

However, some special files may be set up to be filed chronologically, for instance:

- vouchers or receipts which are issued by date
- birth or death certificates
- examination results filed by date of examination.

Test your knowledge and understanding

1   Write down each of the following numbers neatly and accurately. Then put them into numerical order.

58029	68179	32098	51029
38409	28510	30299	43840

2   The following folders have been put on your desk in alphabetical order. You have to put them into numerical order. Change the list so that it is correct.

Sloan C	798	Smythe J	430
Slowe E	6019	Snape A	5201
Smalley A	5883	Snowden G	6102
Smalley J	901	Solanski T	5591
Smith C	2098	Spera V	4889

3   An untrained administrator has put a set of documents into a folder without sorting them into date order. Bearing in mind the *most recent* document should be on the top, identify the order in which you would place these documents into the folder (i.e. oldest first).

Letter dated 25 February

Memo dated 12 January

Letter dated 27 February

E-mail dated 28 February

Letter dated 12 January

Memo dated 1 March

Using indexes

An index is a method of helping you to find something quickly. The index in this book summarises all the topics you may wish to find and refers you to the page number on which you will find each one.

Your supervisor or tutor may suggest you index your NVQ portfolio to help your assessor or verifier find your evidence more quickly. In this case, you would separate the contents of your NVQ portfolio with dividers and then put a summary of the contents at the front.

In a filing system, an index is a method of helping you to find files quickly. You don't need an index for an alphabetical system because it is **direct**. You just go to a cabinet and look under the correct letter of the alphabet to find the file you want.

You can't do this with a numerical system because you are unlikely to know each number. All you know is the name.

The index summarises this information for you. You look in the index under the name and then read across to find the number. A numerical filing system is therefore **indirect**. You find the file in two stages – first by looking in the index, then by going to the filing cabinet.

There are several systems available but these are the ones you are most likely to find.

- A **card index box**. The cards give space on which to write additional information. Guide cards separate the different letters of the alphabet.

- A **strip index**. These are small strips of card which slot into a holder.

Sandford Supplies	5089

- A **rotary index**. These hold small cards which are turned or flipped and can easily fit onto a desk.

- A **visible edge index**. These are quite large cards kept in a flat drawer. The bottom edge displays the important information.

- An **index book**, which has separate pages for each letter of the alphabet.

The big danger is losing an index card or – even worse – the whole index book! A book should be fastened or attached so that it cannot be moved.

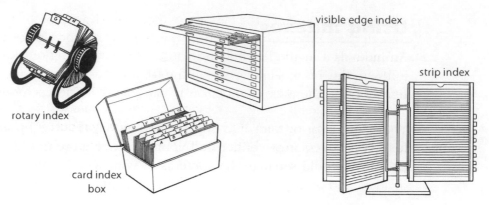

Different index systems

To use the index:

- find out the exact name you need
- locate the name using the alphabetical method
- make a note of the number
- find the file by looking for that number in the filing system.

Remember, if you use a card or strip system *never* remove the card or strip and walk away with it! Remember the number – or write it down on your notebook.

Check it out!

Many small rotary systems are used for the rapid storage and retrieval of telephone numbers.

Obtain a set of small cards yourself (ask your tutor or supervisor) and write on these the name and telephone number of five people you know. If you prefer, you can invent the names and numbers.

If you are working in a group, put all your cards together.

Now decide whether they should be stored alphabetically or numerically (by telephone number) and give a reason for your choice.

Finally, see how quickly you can *accurately* put them into the correct order (both ways!).

Information update

Many organisations use computers to help them to organise their filing. Some keep their index system on a computer database, so you can quickly find the number by typing in the name. Another system incorporates a bar code on every file folder. The files are 'swiped' into and out of the system when they are borrowed so a computer log shows the location of any file at any moment.

The ultimate, of course, is a system where all the documents are scanned into the system and held on computer with special software which allows the documents to be indexed properly. This dramatically reduces the amount of storage space required as thousands of documents can be stored on one optical disk.

Keeping files safe

There are four golden rules.

- Never take documents out of files. If someone wants to borrow a file then lend the *whole* file – or photocopy the document.
- Never take a file out of the system and leave it lying around. Find what you want and put it away again.
- *Never* guess where to put a file. If you aren't certain, ask someone.
- Find out which filing cabinets must be kept locked when there is no one in the office and where the keys must be stored.

If you follow these rules there is less danger of losing a file. However, you also need to learn how to use files properly so you don't damage them.

Again there are four golden rules.

- When you are removing a file folder, grasp it properly and lift it out. *Don't* tug it out by its labelled tab at the top. If the file is heavy, this will break off.
- Don't squash a folder into a drawer or cupboard where there isn't enough space.
- Make sure you put a file into the proper compartment. This is very important if you have pockets in a drawer which the folders could drop in between.

Always put papers neatly in a file

- Put papers into a file properly. This means:
  - there should be no paperclips or pins (which can 'hook' other documents) – staple the documents instead
  - any torn papers should be mended with sticky tape first
  - the documents should be hole punched *squarely* in the middle, otherwise they will be messy in the folder. If you have a punch with a guide ruler then use this, or *gently* fold the paper in half and line up your crease mark with the arrow in the centre of the punch.

Finding and returning files

Both finding and returning files should be done promptly for the following reasons.

- If you are asked to find a file, then it is likely that whoever asked you to do this wants to look at it urgently.
- If you are regularly asked for files, then you can easily forget one or two unless you write every request down. It is easier to get the file immediately.
- If you have any problems finding a file, it is important you tell the appropriate person promptly. If you have delayed doing the job you may not find out until sometime later.
- A file must be returned promptly because other people will want to use it.

Most organisations have a system for booking out files which are borrowed by people. This is dealt with on page 136.

Confidential information and filing

Confidential information refers to information which should not be made available to everyone because it concerns personal or 'sensitive' information about a colleague or customer.

You would be right to be upset if you found out that someone knew where you lived, how much you earned, what happened at your last review or all about your family because a personal file had been left open in the office. Therefore, if you deal with personal or 'sensitive' information at any time you must treat it differently. So:

- never discuss what you read with other people
- don't leave papers lying on your desk
- don't leave the file on your desk
- don't take the file into any public area, such as reception

- don't lend the file to anyone without permission from your supervisor or team leader
- make sure you put the file away after you have used it
- always lock the cabinet and put the key in the proper place if you have been told to do this.

Evidence collection

You need to prove to your assessor that you understand everything you have just read and can apply it at work. The easiest way to do this is to write a short account.

1   Describe the filing system you use and who you need to ask to obtain permission to use it. Say whether it is alphabetical or numerical and describe the type of files which are stored in the system.

2   Describe the equipment you have and say why you think it is important that:
    a   the files must always be kept neat and tidy
    b   that documents are always filed promptly.
    Explain how you organise your work to help to achieve this.

3   Describe any indexing systems that you work with and say how these operate and how you use them.

4   Explain what actions you take:
    a   to make sure files and their contents are not lost or damaged
    b   to make sure files are found and returned promptly.

5   a   Explain what you understand by the term 'confidential information'.
    b   Describe the precautions you would take if you had to deal with a file which contained this type of information.

Element 04.1

Find files

You can expect to be asked to find files by a number of people. You may even want to find files yourself to answer queries. This element is concerned with finding files and following the correct procedures when you do this.

Filing procedures

There are some common sense rules relating to finding files which you must follow:

- only look for – and pass on – files you are allowed to handle. If you are asked for a confidential file, ask for your supervisor's permission
- understand how your system works, so that you can find a file easily without rummaging or disrupting the contents of the whole cabinet.
- know how to find a file which could be in more than one place. Normally it will be **cross-referenced**. This means that you will find a card in the place you are looking which directs you to the right place, for example:

> **CROSS REFERENCE CARD**
> For UCL see
> University College of London

- know the system used to record files which are borrowed by people.

Noting a file has been removed

If you have a very neat and tidy system, you may not like the idea of removing or lending out files to people in case they get lost. However, the main point of keeping documents is so that people can refer to them. If you refuse to let anyone borrow anything then there is little point in keeping the papers in the first place!

There are two systems which may be used to note down that a file has been removed.

A file diary

This tracks all file movements – either on paper or on computer. It identifies which files have been taken from the cabinet and checks these back when they are returned. It is used when files are very important and when losing them could be very serious. Often borrowers have to sign for the files they take.

Absent system

A more common system is one which records files which have been lent. If someone wants to borrow a file you must:

- make a note of the file, the person who has borrowed it and the date
- ask the borrower when he or she expects to return the file
- remind the borrower (politely) if it hasn't been returned by this date.

In some organisations, you complete an 'absent card' and put this in place of the file. This is a good idea because anyone who goes to find the file then sees immediately where it is.

Under normal circumstances you would:

- locate the file
- note it has been removed
- pass it on to the person who wants it
- check it is returned.

Test your knowledge and understanding

1   The best way to understand cross referencing is to use the *Yellow Pages*. The designers have assumed that people may look for certain headings in various ways – and have tried to think of all the alternatives. They have then put a cross-reference in at each of these points to refer the reader to the correct section. They also include a reference where additional information may be useful in a different section. For example, if you want to rent a flat you look under 'rented accommodation'. Here you will be directed to estate agents.

Now find each of the following telephone numbers using your *Yellow Pages*. Find the entry (using the normal alphabetical system), then follow any cross-referencing information, then find the correct number:

a   your local job centre

b   a personal trainer

c   a sailing club

d   a nail technician

e   a theme park.

2   Copy the table on page 138 onto a clean page. Then assume you have lent out each of the following files this morning and make the correct entry.

a   Tracey Jones asks to borrow the file on Peter Brown. She says she will return it tomorrow.

b   Bill Watson wants the file on John Sykes until next Monday.

c   Tracey brings Peter Brown's file back and says it's the wrong one. She wants the file on Peter S Brown.

d   Asif Mehrban asks you for the file on Craven Garage. He wants it until tomorrow.

e   Aled Baron wants the file on Broughton Services until tomorrow.

f   Ten minutes later Aled brings it back again.

Date	Name of file borrower	Name of	Date to be returned	✓ when returned

Dealing with problems

The biggest problem is when a file suddenly goes missing, there is no record of it being borrowed and it is required urgently. At this stage normally everyone has to help find it.

First, tell your supervisor or team leader immediately. You may even find that they have borrowed it!

Helping to finding a missing file

The most useful action you can take is to:

- recheck the book to make sure you haven't missed the entry which says it has been borrowed
- look on top of the filing cabinet
- look on top of desks in the area
- *think* about who *may* have borrowed it – sometimes the topic or the name is a clue if you know who deals with this type of work or this customer
- if you have a vertical cabinet, check the file hasn't slid between two suspension pockets
- ask people if they have seen it
- think about whether there is any similar name the file could have been stored under
- if you use a numerical system, try obvious number transpositions, e.g. 5808 could be filed under 8508 or 8805.

Other types of problems

Other problems you may encounter include:

- a folder so full it is bursting apart
- so many folders in a drawer or cabinet you can't get them in any more
- some borrowers never returning a file on time – when you have documents to put into it.

You should mention obvious problems to either a senior colleague or your team leader. In each of the above cases, however, the solution is slightly different.

- A folder which is overflowing needs the documents dividing between two folders. Label each one with the date the file was started and, in the case of the first folder, the date it was completed.

- A drawer or cabinet which is overflowing needs 'pruning'. In other words, excess documents or old files need moving out. They may be thrown away or transferred into a basement area. Ordinary documents are often thrown away but if you work for a solicitor, for example, client files are kept for several years in a basement area after they cease to be 'active'.

  However, always remember that you should only do this under the express instructions from your supervisor.

- A borrower who 'hoards' a file may have to 'lend it back' for a short time so that you can update it.

Evidence collection

1 Keep a record of files you have to find over a period of time, such as a month or two. You have to prove you can find files which are stored *both* alphabetically and numerically. An easy way is to copy out the table below and complete it.

Identify the storage method by ticking the correct box.

When you have finished your record, ask your supervisor or team leader to sign it to prove it is true.

2 If you encounter any problems finding a file, make a note of these and state what happened and who you reported the problem to. Again, ask this person to sign your account to prove it is true.

Date	Name of file	Required by	Storage method	
			Alphabetical	Numerical

Update and store files

Another frequent job is to put documents into the correct files to update them and to store the files safely again. Again, you are likely to find specific procedures in place which state how you should do this.

Adding new items to a file

Documents for filing are normally placed in a filing tray. It is always better if filing is done very frequently, preferably daily.

Many organisations have a special 'release mark' on a document which means it can be filed. This may be a simple 'tick' that your supervisor or team leader puts on a document when it has been dealt with. If you work for an employer which uses this system, do query any document put in the filing tray which does *not* have a release mark.

Pre-sorting routines

It is better to pre-sort a pile of documents first. This means grouping them. For instance:

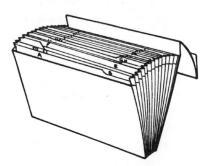

- you can use an expanding concertina file to separate documents into alphabetical order

- if you have a numerical system, you can start by putting the number on each one, if this is not part of your reference system

Concertina files can be useful to sort documents

- you can then put documents which must go in the same file together, in date order, with the latest date on top.

You then reduce the time you need to take moving between one file and another.

Storing the file

Once you have punched the documents correctly and put them neatly into the file, you need to make sure that the file is returned to its proper place as soon as possible.

Health and safety: a final note

You should know from studying Unit 102 that health and safety applies to all areas of work in an office – including filing. The main points to bear in mind when you are filing include:

- never leaving open cabinet drawers (particularly the bottom one!) for people to fall over
- never carrying so many files or folders you can't see where you are going
- never arranging for a filing cabinet to be placed near a door – so that either the person entering a room or the person working at the filing cabinet would be at risk
- using a safety stool if you have to reach into a tall lateral cupboard.

You should note that modern filing cabinets are designed with an anti-tilt mechanism so that only one drawer will open at once.

However, all cabinets are still safer if heavy items are in the bottom drawer for stability (not two folders and your coffee mug!).

Evidence collection

Keep a record of the work you do in updating and storing files over a month or two. Again you must prove you can update and store files in both an alphabetical and a numerical system.

You may find it useful to copy out and use the table below. Then ask your supervisor or team leader to sign it to confirm it is true.

Date	Name of file updated	Storage system		✓ if index used
		Alphabetical	Numerical	

Unit 105 Enter and find data using a computer

> This unit is one of two Optional Group A units. You need to do *either* this unit *or* unit 104 to gain your award, but not both.

This unit is concerned with how you:

- enter data on a computer
- find data on a computer.

It is **important** because:

- virtually all business organisations use computers to store data
- most administrators use computers as a basic part of their job
- if you use a computer you will need to enter and find data regularly
- developing your IT skills is a good way of furthering your career prospects.

There are two elements to this unit. Before you start these, you need to understand the main reasons why computers are used in business and some basic facts about entering and finding data.

Special note

This unit has been written with instructions for using Microsoft Office 2000 software, i.e. Word 2000, Excel 2000 and Access 2000. If you are not sure whether you are using Windows software you can check by seeing if there is a Desktop with icons on your screen when you start your computer. If you are not using Windows or are using an earlier version of Microsoft Office or different software entirely, then please see your tutor or supervisor about converting the specific commands given in this unit.

Key skills signpost

If you are taking your Key Skills award in Problem Solving at level 1, then you can develop your knowledge of using a computer and use the information given in this unit to help you to obtain evidence for your Key Skills portfolio.

You have two problems to solve in relation to using your computer system. These are described below.

1   You are very aware of the Data Protection Act, especially as you often handle customer information. You are often asked for print-outs and asked to leave these on your desk for people to collect, sometimes after you have gone home. Sometimes they are never collected – at other times you have to check as to who actually obtained the data. Last week two folders containing customer print-outs disappeared off your desk but everyone says they have not seen them. You are concerned that this is breaching security and would like a different system for issuing the data you have been asked for.

2   You get on well with most of your team but one member of staff often asks you to input data or find data without giving you clear instructions or explaining the job to you. This means it takes you twice as long to do his work as anyone else's. Yesterday you did your best to find what he wanted but, in the end, gave him the wrong data. This morning he has been very curt with you and was heard saying you need to improve your computer skills. You feel this is unfair and want to solve the problem but aren't certain what to do.

Alternatively, your supervisor or tutor may wish to help you identify a different problem relating to using your computer which you could tackle.

PS1.1   Arrange a meeting with your supervisor or tutor at which you agree the problem and decide the best way to go about tackling it.

After the meeting, write a description of the problem yourself. Suggest at least *two* ways in which it could be solved. Then consider which of your ideas are likely to be the most successful.

PS1.2   Arrange another meeting with your supervisor or tutor at which you can discuss your suggestions.

Decide how you will try out your plan and what you will do next. Write a short account of what was agreed and the steps you must now take to try to solve *both* problems.

Carry out your plan and make notes about the result.

PS1.3   Check if the problem has now been solved.

Write a short account of the results of your actions.

Explain what you have learned from this which would help you to improve your approach to problem solving in the future.

Enter and find data using a computer

Most administrators use a computer as part of their work. They may also use different types of software, such as the following.

- A **word processing package** to create documents, such as memos and letters. Examples include Word and WordPerfect.

- A **spreadsheet package** in which they enter text and numbers into a worksheet. Numbers are a key aspect of a spreadsheet as many different types of calculations can be carried out. The text in a spreadsheet is usually entered to describe what the numbers represent. Examples include Excel, Quattro and Lotus 1,2,3.

- A **database** which holds any type of information that is regularly used by the organisation, such as customer or supplier records. Examples include Access, Dbase and Paradox.

Although you can use any type of software to achieve this unit, you will find that you must know something about databases as part of the knowledge and understanding requirements.

Check it out!

If you are using Windows-based software it is important you know the main terms used. Check on your screen and with your supervisor or tutor that you are familiar with all the terms shown on the next page.

You also need to know the term **dialogue box.** This appears when you select an option from the menu bar and then click on a command from the drop-down menu but additional information must then be supplied. For example, if you select File and then New. The dialogue box then asks you to identify the type of document you wish to create in the box.

An example of a dialogue box is shown on page 161.

Tool bar
This contains **icons** – or small pictures – which represent quick methods of accessing an option you use regularly.

Title bar
The top bar on your screen which shows the software you are using.

Menu bar
The next bar gives you menus from which you can choose commands. Clicking on an item gives you a **drop-down menu** with the options. If an option is followed by . . . this means that additional choices are available (e.g. File then Open . . .)

Maximise button/Minimise button
These increase or reduce the size of your active window to take up the whole of your desktop or reduce it to a smaller size.

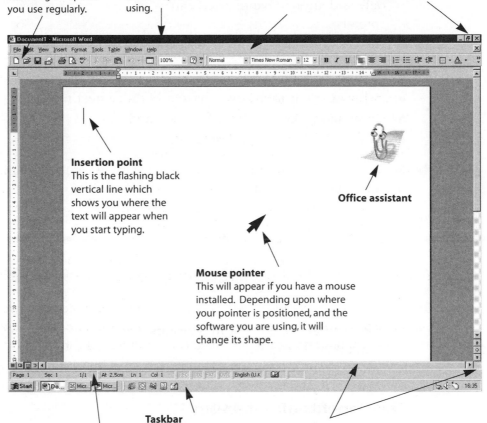

Insertion point
This is the flashing black vertical line which shows you where the text will appear when you start typing.

Office assistant

Mouse pointer
This will appear if you have a mouse installed. Depending upon where your pointer is positioned, and the software you are using, it will change its shape.

Status bar
This provides details of your current status, e.g. the page you are on and the position of your insertion point.

Taskbar
This shows the Windows applications you are currently using. The taskbar can be hidden if you prefer and you can access Start by pressing the Windows key on your keyboard.

Scroll bars
These are at the bottom and side of your screen and help you to move through a document. You can drag the **scroll box** to move through your document page by page. The **scroll arrows** are useful as you can click on these to move steadily through a document line by line.

A Windows screen looks like this

Why databases are used

A database can be described as a very large electronic filing system, on a particular subject or topic. It is organised – or structured – so that you can find anything you need relatively easily. For example:

- you could store the names, addresses, telephone numbers and birthdays of your friends in a database
- you could list your CD collection in a database under the title of the CD and artist or band.

In both cases, you could design the database so that at the press of a key (or two) you could find out:

- the phone number of any friend
- which of your friends will have a birthday next month
- how many CDs you have for one band
- which CD you bought last.

Remember, these are only examples. A database can be organised to quickly identify any other type of information which is regularly needed; for example, supermarkets use their customer database to find out which types of products individual customers prefer to buy.

Check it out!

Nowadays most mobile phones have a 'phone book' facility, so you don't need to remember numbers but you can look them up when you want. These usually also link to *incoming* calls, so that you can identify the caller before you answer. This is an example of a small but useful database.

The benefits of databases

You should already be able to identify a few of these, but it is helpful to look at them from a business perspective.

As an example, imagine you are employed by Haydock Veterinary Clinic. Twelve months ago the staff kept all their records on a paper-based card index system. They wrote the details of all their customers on a small card which looked like this.

HAYDOCK VETERINARY CLINIC

Owner's name:	Sean Donnelly		
Address:	23 Redfern Road, Hightown, HG3 6MP		
Tel No:	01878-484948		
Type of pet:	Dog	Breed:	Golden Retriever
Name of pet:	Winston	DOB:	October 1995
Date of last annual check-up/vaccinations:		12.12.01	

These card records are useful, but they have some limitations.

- Finding a card can be time-consuming, especially if they get out of order.
- Cards can easily get lost or be borrowed from the system and 'go missing'.
- If Sean has several pets, it may be necessary to staple several cards together to hold all the information.
- If staff want to remind customers that their animals are due for their next check-up they must search through *all* the cards to find which ones are due next month. This takes time. They then need to prepare letters separately to each person.

Setting up a simple database

John Haydock, the vet, decides to invest in a computerised database. This is designed to collect exactly the same type of information but to hold it on computer. In this case the card design is virtually the same as the paper version when it is seen on the computer screen.

What happens now? First all the information about each customer and his or her pets has to be entered into a separate database form. When a form is complete it becomes a **record**. Each customer will be a separate record. This process is time-consuming to set up, but after that the system will only have to be kept up to date with new customers (or new pets) added and records amended if necessary.

The staff are delighted with the system for several reasons.

- Cards can no longer get lost.
- The records are quicker to update when someone brings a pet for a routine check-up and vaccination.
- The system can be used by several people at the same time, using different computers.
- The system can answer queries very rapidly. For instance, the staff can 'search' the system to find which customers must bring which of their pets for a check up next month.
- The system can also be linked to other computer software. For instance, a reminder letter can be prepared on a word processing package and the names and addresses of customers can be inserted automatically. This saves a lot of work for the staff.
- The system can be used for other things, e.g.:
  - labels can be prepared for all customers for sending out mailshots such as monthly newsletters
  - customers with a particular type or breed of pet can be found easily if John Haydock wants to contact them for a specific reason

– the system can be extended to include other items, for instance, which customers owe money on their accounts so that reminder letters can be sent.

Basic terms in a database

A lot of work goes into the design and construction of databases. There are also special terms relating to databases which you need to know.

The table below summarises all the terms you need to know for reference. However, you will find many of these terms easier to understand when you have completed this section of the unit.

Database terms	
Form	A form is a blank database record for one set of information.
Record	This is a completed database form – when the details have been added. Each customer has his/her own record.
Field	A field is the space where you can enter data. It has a title before it which shows the type of data required, e.g. First name or Town. Fields vary in length and also vary in relation to the type of data to be entered (e.g. text or numbers). In some databases, the designers will help to ensure only the correct type of data is entered, e.g. in a 'money' field the database will not accept a text entry.
Data	This is the information entered into a field.
Index	A database index is one method of quickly finding information. It is similar to the index at the back of this book as it lists key words you may want to find quickly.
Key words	These are the most important words which relate to a database and which may be used to construct an index.
Key data	This is important data which is normally put into a special field. It is normally unique to each record. For instance, customers may have the same surname or first name, or even live at the same address – so this can't be *unique* data. Examples of unique data include: student ID numbers, customer reference numbers and bank account numbers. They are different for each record. If you know the key data it is easy to find a record quickly.
Key field	The field which holds the key data.
Reference code	An abbreviated method of writing a key word or key data.
Table	The complete database. Many databases are created as a table, with vertical columns and horizontal rows. If you are searching for data you are likely to do this in a table.
Report	A list of specific information extracted from a database, set out so that the different categories are easy to read.

Test your knowledge and understanding

The illustration below shows a database record for one of John Haydock's customers. After you have studied the database terms on page 148, look at this and see if you can identify:

a a field

b one example of data

c the only data which is *unique* to Ken Franks' record

d the field that must therefore be the key field.

Check your answers with your tutor or supervisor before you read any further.

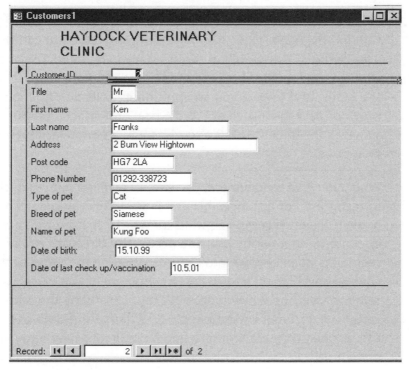

A database record

Check it out!

Indexes and key words become much easier to understand if you find some examples of how they are used.

Start by looking at the index at the back of this book. This is constructed from key words, i.e. words you may use to look up a particular topic. You would then read across to the page number and find the page you want. On a computer, you would normally click on the key word and then click or double click to find out more about that topic.

Each of the following is an example of a computerised index. Investigate at least *three* of them on your own computer system and see how they work to help you find what you need.

1   The menu bar at the top of your Windows screen is comprised of key words (see below). When you click on one of these words you access a drop down menu. You can think of this as a miniature index. Note that those followed by dots provide you with additional options e.g. New . . . or Open . . . on your File menu.

   This type of key words and index system is designed to help you to find the options you want quickly and easily.

2   If you access your on-line help facility then, if you use Office 2000, you will find the paper-clip Office Assistant on screen. You can then type in a key word to help you find the assistance you need. This is a quite a sophisticated type of index system as the program searches through the index itself to give you an appropriate selection to choose from. In previous packages (such as Word 6 or WordPerfect 7) clicking Help provides the full index but also gives you a search facility as well (see next page).

3   When you save a document, you should give it a name which is easy to recognise. For instance, this unit is saved on computer under the name '105unit'. This is a key word (or words). If you save your documents on a floppy disk and access the directory you are really seeing an index of key words. You can change the order of these in various ways to help you to find the document you want. Your normal options are by name, by type of file, by size and by the date you last saved the document. Most people find 'name' and 'date' the most useful when they are trying to find a document they have saved previously.

4   If you use e-mail at work or at college then you may have an address book facility. You can store the names, addresses and e-mail addresses of your regular contacts. The address book is an excellent example of a database. You will also normally have the facility to bring up your address book on screen and/or a list of your contacts (see next page).

A File drop down menu is like a miniature index

WordPerfect Help index

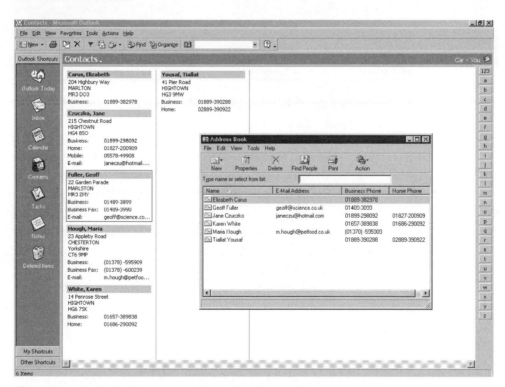

The address book facility is a good example of a database

Information update

Web site and web page designers use a variety of tactics to help people find data they want quickly and easily. They use key words, indexes and search facilities. They also use the 'split screen' technique regularly so that you have two panes of information. One may give you an index which remains on your screen whilst the other pane changes depending upon the word you select.

On many sites you will see key words across the top (like your menu bar), as well as an index facility and a search facility. Hyperlinks are another way of helping you to move quickly to data you want – either to another part of that web site or another web site altogether. You know when you are on a hyperlink because you see a 'hand' icon when you move your mouse pointer over it.

Below is an illustration of the Heinemann Vocational NVQ web page. You can see the index, search facilities and links which have been included to help users find the data they want.

If you have Internet access, see how this system operates on other sites. Good ones to try include www.bbc.co.uk, www.royalmail.com, www.microsoft.com, www.waterstones.co.uk. Access these and then see if you can find three web sites yourself which offer this facility.

An example of a web page

Instructions for inputting and finding data

Whether you are keying in data, or finding data which has already been entered into any software package, you need to know:

- what you must input
- where you must enter the data
- what data you need to find

- where this data is likely to be
- the file or record into which the data has been saved originally.

The more precise your instructions, the easier the task – and the less chance of a mistake being made.

The main points to bear in mind are as follows.
- You should know which type of software you are supposed to be using, e.g. spreadsheet, database or word processing package.
- Check you understand the terms used for the documents created by different software packages.
  - If you are word processing, then you will be working with documents.
  - If you are using a spreadsheet package, then you will be working with worksheets.
  - If you are using a database, then you are likely to be working with forms, records and reports.
- If you are adding data to an existing document, worksheet or database, you need to know how to find this and bring it up on screen.
- You now need to make sure you know exactly what data you must input or find. This reduces the chances of you keying in the wrong data or spending ages looking for data because you're not sure what you are looking for.

Note that further information on inputting and finding data is given on pages 159–162.

Asking for guidance

It is important to ask for help when you need it.

Jessica has just started work at John Haydock's veterinary practice. At her interview, John and Cathie, the administrator, were pleased when Jessica said she was good at using her own initiative to solve problems. She is now determined to prove that she can do this.

Today Cathie is having a day off. Before surgery, John asked Jessica to unpack three boxes of pet accessories and put some items on display in reception and the rest in the storeroom. He asked her to add these new items to the price list kept on reception and, then to print out a list of the next day's appointments. He then went into the surgery to see several waiting clients.

Jessica unpacks the boxes. She finds an invoice in one of them which lists all the items and the amount owing for the goods. She then asks the receptionist for the old price list. Jessica sits at her computer and starts to type this using her word processing package. She adds the items she has just unpacked and refers to the invoice for the prices. She is pleased with her work even though it has taken her all morning. After lunch she decides to tackle the appointments list. She has no idea how to do this but decides there must be a note in the client files so she starts to get these out

of the filing cabinets. By 3 o'clock she is surrounded by files but hasn't found one with an appointment for tomorrow. At this point John Haydock walks back into the office.

Test your knowledge and understanding

Answer the questions below before you read the section which follows.

1 What do you think John Haydock's reaction will be when he sees Jessica surrounded by files? Give a reason for your answer.

2 What do you think John Haydock's reaction will be when he reads the price list Jessica has prepared? Again, give a reason for your answer.

3 Do you think Jessica could have saved herself time and effort when she prepared the price list?

4 Why was it important she asked for guidance before she entered the prices?

5 Why was it important she asked for guidance about preparing the appointments list?

6 Jessica tried hard – she wanted to prove she could use her own initiative, which is admirable. However, there are times when this is not advisable. Can you suggest three occasions when it is much better to ask for guidance?

Solving problems with data

Jessica had several problems but she made things worse by not checking a few obvious facts.

- If the price list is kept on reception, it was probably prepared on computer. It should therefore be saved and can be recalled and quickly updated.

- Jessica used the invoices for the prices, but this gives the price John Haydock *pays* for the items, not the amount he charges for them. Jessica does not know how much he charges so *must* ask either him or Cathie to obtain this information.

- Jessica had never prepared an appointments list before – yet one is obviously prepared every day, so there must be a quick and easy way of doing this. She needs to find out what it is!

- Jessica has spent all day doing two jobs which could have taken less than half an hour if she had only asked for guidance first.

Always ask for guidance:

- if you are not sure about the data to input
- if the data you have been given is unclear
- if your data is incomplete
- when you don't have the data you need
- when you don't know what to do as you haven't done it before
- when you cannot find something on your computer system.

Jessica was sensible when she asked the receptionist for the price list. Identifying *who* to ask is important. She didn't want to worry John Haydock, but in Cathie's absence he was the only person who could have given her the information she needed. When you are given a job you need to identify who is the best person to help you solve different types of queries, for instance:

- who to ask for help about your computer system
- who to ask for help about finding data
- who to ask if your data is incomplete, unclear or missing.

It is unlikely that these will be the same people!

Check it out!

Understanding tables is important whichever software you are using. If you are word processing you may create a table in which to enter text and numbers. If you are entering data into a spreadsheet then you are working with a very large table – a worksheet. If you are using a database, you may need to recall the table including *all* the data in the database.

For this reason, you need to check you understand how tables are constructed and the key words that are used to refer to them.

Check it out! *continued*

- *Every* type of table is constructed of **cells**. These are the small boxes into which you enter either text or numbers.
- A **column** is the name for a vertical line of boxes.
- A **row** is the name for a horizontal line of boxes.

In a spreadsheet the columns each have a letter and the rows a number. You always refer to the letter first, e.g. A10, C12 etc. to name a cell. In all Windows software, clicking on a cell will make it the **active cell**. Your active cell is the one where your insertion point is, so you can enter text or numbers into it. You can tell, because it will be surrounded by a black rectangle. The name of the active cell is always shown in a box at the top left. You can quickly move to a cell by entering its name in this box.

Test your knowledge and understanding

1 Compare the two illustrations on page 157. One is a simple table produced in Word, the other is a spreadsheet. On *both* of these, make sure you can identify:

   a a column   **b** a row   **c** a cell.

2 Use the spreadsheet illustration to answer the following questions:

   a Which is the active cell?

   b Which cell contains the information E100W?

   c Which cell contains the information brown (C5 envelopes)?

   d If you wanted to make H4 the active cell, what would you do?

   e What might happen if you wanted to move to cell P50?

   Check your answer with your tutor.

3 Now practise asking for guidance by checking with your tutor or supervisor if you are unsure about undertaking any of the following operations when you are entering text or numbers into a table, using whichever type of software you normally use for inputting or finding data in a table:

   - changing the width of a column
   - changing the height of a row
   - adding a new row or column
   - deleting a row or a column
   - joining cells together.

	January	February	March
Bookings received	567	609	403
Bookings confirmed	551	587	400

A simple table in Word

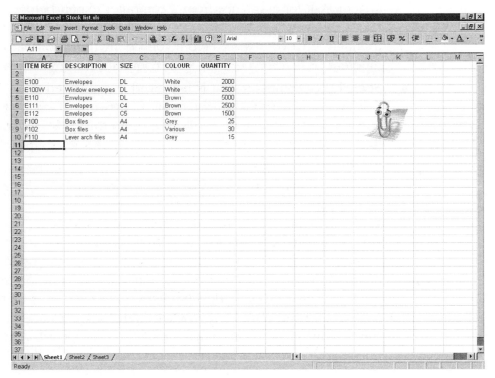

A spreadsheet in Excel

Protecting data

If you use a computer then you may have certain worries about the documents you create.

- Are they safe?
- Are they secure?
- What would happen if your system 'went down'?
- What would happen if a file was corrupted so that you could no longer access it?
- What would happen if you lost a floppy disk with important documents stored on it?

Computer failure and corruption of data can cause enormous problems. So, too, can human failings – such as deleting an important computer file by accident or losing a floppy disk! For that reason, all organisations have procedures to help to prevent such problems.

- **Safety** of data is improved if you routinely 'back up' all your computer data. The most usual method is to copy files saved on your hard disk onto a floppy disk. However, you need to label your floppy disks carefully and keep them safely – in a proper disk box.

  You should have your automatic back-up facility set so that your work is routinely backed-up every few minutes by your computer system. Ask for assistance from a computer expert before you try to check this yourself. You will also have fewer problems if you routinely save your work before you do anything complicated, different or before you leave your computer for any length of time.

- **Security** of computer data is improved if authorised users have to 'log on' using a special user ID and a password. If you use a computer in a college you will have to do this. It is *very* important that you never tell anyone your password or you completely destroy the whole idea of security!

  You should take sensible precautions yourself – by switching off your computer when you are not working on it and especially when you are leaving the office – even for only a short time. There should also be security precautions to prevent computer viruses from being introduced into the system. This includes not allowing staff to use their own floppy disks and having anti-virus software on the system to prevent viruses being downloaded via the Internet. A useful tip, if you have e-mail, is never to download anything from an unknown source which has an attachment urging you to open it immediately! Check with your tutor first.

Information update

A virus is a rogue computer program which 'spreads' throughout a computer system disabling files, flashing up weird messages on your screen and even erasing all the data stored on your hard disk drive.

Most of the viruses which you read about in the press have been downloaded from the Internet as an e-mail attachment. Virtually all organisations have anti-virus software installed on their computer systems. If you have a computer at home which isn't protected then you need to investigate your options. For less than £30 you could buy Norton AntiVirus or McAfee VirusScan and save yourself a lot of worry – especially if you regularly use the Internet.

Timescales for inputting and finding data

How long it takes you to input and find data will depend upon:

- whether you have done the job before
- the length and complexity of the data
- whether you are simply updating a previous document or creating a new one
- how much information you are given to help you.

You can normally sense when things are going wrong because a job is taking you too long! In this case, ask for help and make sure that anyone who is depending upon you to complete the task quickly is also informed.

Inputting and finding data using different software

Before you start to input or find data you need to know how to:

- use your computer system and load the software
- create a new document or worksheet
- open an existing file
- find a file or record which has been saved previously
- move around your screen.

Starting your system

The way in which you start your system and load the software you use will vary, depending mainly on whether your workplace or college has a networked computer system or whether you are using a stand-alone PC.

- On a networked system you will have to log in, using your ID and password.
- On a stand-alone system you will switch on and Windows will load automatically. You may have been able to select a password which must be keyed in before the desktop will appear.

Normally your system will be devised so that you will see your Windows desktop with icons representing the software you use regularly. Simply double-click on the icon you want. If you can't see an icon for your software, click on the Start button to see other options and look there. If you see the name listed, scroll your mouse pointer up to highlight it and then click the left mouse button.

Creating a new document or worksheet

All Microsoft office packages enable you to do this in the same way.

You can use the Menu bar *or* click on the small icon on the Formatting toolbar. To use the menu bar, click on File then choose New. If you prefer to use the icons then click on the icon for the blank paper. If you are using Word, then you will see the New dialogue box and will have the option to choose from a blank document or several other types. Generally you will be choosing a blank document.

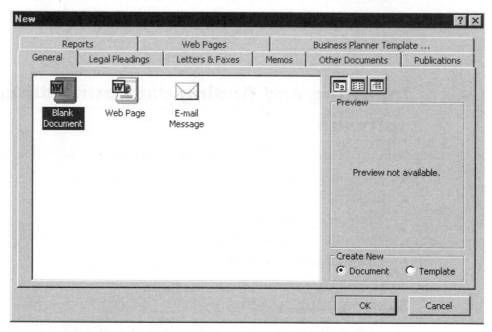

Creating a new document in Word

Opening an existing file

Remember that you find a computer file by searching for the name under which it has been saved. You also need to know *where* the file has been saved.

Start by clicking File on your Menu bar and then selecting Open. Or click on the open folder icon on the formatting toolbar. The Open dialogue box will now appear on your screen.

Now decide which drive to look in. Clicking on the right hand arrow opposite the Look In window gives you all your options. If, for instance, the file was on a floppy disk you would now load this and click on **a:**. A list of documents you have saved on this disk would now be listed on screen. You can double click on the one you want, or click on it and then click on Open at the bottom right.

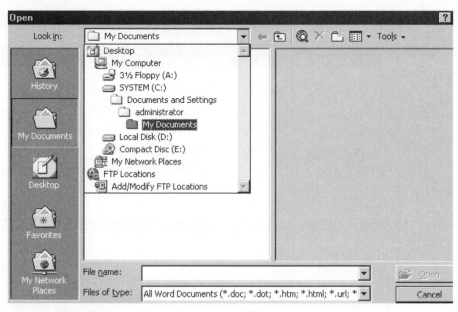

An Open file dialogue box

Finding a file

It is easy to open an existing file if you know the drive on which it was stored and the name. If you do not, then you need to know how to find a file.

With the Open dialogue box on screen, click the downward arrow to the right of your Tools option. Then select the icon showing the binoculars. You will then see the Find binoculars on your screen. Click on this to bring up the Find dialogue box.

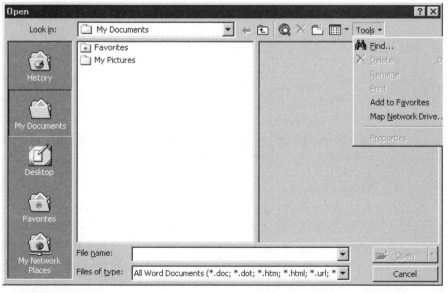

The Find screen

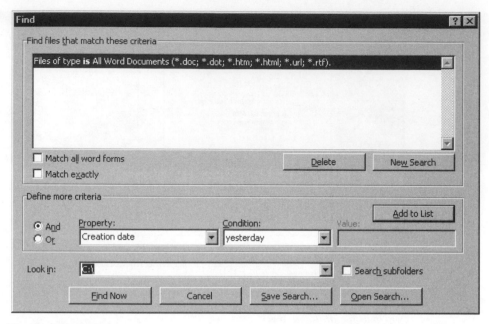

The Find dialogue box

You have several options to choose. If you look under 'Property', for instance, you can search on a keyword, on the creation date or on the file title – to name just a few. The 'Condition' varies depending upon which property you choose. Using Find takes a little getting used to at first, but it is worth mastering if you regularly need to find saved files on your system. Again, remember to ask for guidance if you need it!

Moving around your screen

You do this by using a combination of the keys on your keyboard and your mouse.

- **Your keyboard**
  Many of the keys have been designed to help you to move around quickly and easily. There will also be useful shortcuts in your software program you should know, too. The chart on the next page includes the major keys you should use regularly to move around your screen and your document.

- **Your mouse**
  Your mouse has two buttons. It may also have a wheel in the middle (which helps you to scroll quickly through a document) as well as a ball underneath. You need to understand the difference between:
  - a single click of the left button
  - a double click of the left button

- a right click (ie clicking the right button once)
- and how to drag using your mouse. In this case you put the arrow (the mouse pointer) over an object on screen and then press and hold the left mouse button. Now move the mouse to where you want an object to be – holding the button all the time – and then release the left button.

KEYS TO HELP YOU MOVE AROUND YOUR DOCUMENT

Arrow keys	Use these to quickly move through a document – up and down a line at a time, or to the left and right a character at a time.
End	Will take you immediately to the end of the line.
Page up	Takes you to the previous screen.
Page down	Takes you to the next screen when you are in the middle of a document

USEFUL COMBINATION KEYS

Ctrl+right arrow	Takes you to the next word.
Ctrl+left arrow	Takes you to the previous word.
Ctrl+end	Takes you to the end of the document.
Ctrl+Home	Takes you to the beginning of the document.

EDITING TEXT

Backspace	Deletes the character (or selected text) to the *left* of your insertion point.
Delete	Deletes the character (or selected text) to the *right* of your insertion point.

SELECTING TEXT

- Select a single word by double-clicking on it.
- Select specific text by pointing to the first character and then dragging the insertion point to the last character. Then release the mouse button. If you get this wrong, click anywhere in your document to start again.
- Select all the text by clicking on the Edit menu and selecting Select All.

Entering and finding data

This is covered in elements 105.1 and 105.2 on pages 166 to 173.

Check it out!

1   Check that you can easily start your computer system and access the software you are using without any difficulty.

2   Check that you can easily open a 'new' document (or worksheet) or open an existing document using both your menu bar options *and* the icons on your formatting toolbar.

3   With a document, worksheet or database record on screen, practise moving around using your keyboard properly.

4   Find out the difference between your left and right mouse buttons by pointing at various options on screen and pressing first the left button and then the right. You will find that you are often given different options when you press the right one.

5   Put a floppy disk with several documents in your a: drive and then practise finding different ones using the Find facility. Ask your tutor or supervisor for guidance if you are having difficulty.

The basic legal requirements for storing data on a computer system

The most important legal requirement is specified in the **Data Protection Act 1998**. This protects all individuals – including you – as it regulates the type of information which organisations can store about people and who they can pass it on to. The main points of this Act are summarised on page 165.

You should note that organisations which collect information about you normally provide a statement on a form you receive, with a box you can tick if you don't want them to pass on your data to anyone else. Normally this statement is in very small print – with a tiny box. The idea is that most people won't see it – which technically means they have given their approval that their data can be passed on!

DATA PROTECTION: KEY FACTS

Data on individuals must be:

- obtained with their consent
- held for a specific purpose
- relevant to the reason for holding it
- accurate
- up-to-date
- stored securely
- kept no longer than is necessary.

Individuals have the right to:

- see the data which is being held on them
- stop organisations passing it on without their consent
- insist inaccurate data is corrected
- claim compensation if they suffer damage or distress because the data was used wrongly.

These regulations do not apply to data:

- held for national security
- kept by the police (e.g. crime records) or Inland Revenue (for tax purposes)
- held for medical, education or social work
- kept for research or statistics (such as the Census data)
- held only by private individuals in their homes (such as your personal address list).

Information update

There are other types of legislation you should note if you regularly use a computer – especially if you use e-mail or the Internet. In this book you have already learned about two – the Display Screen Equipment Regulations and the Data Protection Act. However, it is useful to know that:

- you can break the law if you write and send an e-mail which is malicious about anyone, as this is libel
- you can also create problems if you download information from the Internet and then circulate it as your own, as you are breaking the law on copyright
- you can be prosecuted under the Computer Misuse Act if you access any data stored on a computer system without authorisation – whether or not you intend to do any damage to it
- your employer has the right to monitor how you use your computer – in particular how you use the Internet – and can also read the e-mails you send and receive (see page 98).

Element 105.1 — Enter data on a computer

Entering – or inputting – data is required to produce any document, worksheet or database record. You may be inputting new data or amending existing data.

Inputting data accurately

It is sensible to find out *what* you are supposed to be doing – as this helps you to understand the task. For instance, if someone gives you a list of numbers to put into a table this is meaningless. If someone asks you to put in the mileage distances between your home town and other cities and towns in England you can understand what you are doing. You can also spot obvious errors. If you know you live 100 miles from London and the figure under mileage says 500 you should query it.

Remember that if you have any queries about data you have been given, *always* ask for guidance from the person who gave you the instructions, your line manager, supervisor or team leader.

Identifying and correcting your mistakes

For this unit, you must enter *both* words and numbers. Numbers are always more difficult for two reasons. First, even the cleverest computer program won't be able to check them for you. Secondly, a quick read through afterwards won't help you either! You need to sit down and read them out loud, with a colleague beside you checking the data from the original copy. This is easier if you have prepared a table or entered the data into a spreadsheet. If you are entering numbers into database records you will have to check them yourself, as you go. However, as you saw on page 148, the designers may have put in certain controls to stop you entering text into some number fields.

It helps if you are aware of common errors. For example, it is easy to:

- enter the current year under date of birth by mistake
- miss out a number, especially in a long sequence
- 'hover' over a key, so you repeat a number by mistake, e.g. 28884 instead of 2884.
- transpose a number and type 29873 instead of 28973.

Always, of course, make sure that you *both* spell-check *and* proof-read the words you have entered.

Test your knowledge and understanding

a Suggest the worst possible consequences which could arise from each of the following keying-in mistakes

b Then state what action you would take if you *later* reread each document and saw what you had typed.

1 You input 20 hours overtime for a member of staff who is claiming 28 hours.

2 You type an interview date in a letter as 27 May instead of 26 May.

3 You misread the place of a meeting and type Bedford rather than Bradford.

4 On an order form, you type 1000 boxes of paper instead of 100 boxes.

5 You are sending a memo to staff about a coach trip. Each person must pay £22 but you type £12 in error and everyone pays up promptly.

Information update

Keying-in errors which have catastrophic consequences are often reported in the press. An example of computer error related to Key Skills tests when one awarding body had to apologise to 10,000 students who had taken level 1 and 2 tests in communication, application of number and information technology because the students were given the wrong result. The wrong pass marks were set in the computer and as a result some students were told they had passed IT when they hadn't and many were told they hadn't passed the other two tests when they had!

Mistakes like this are often said to be caused by 'fat finger syndrome' – the accidental pressing of the wrong key on a computer. They are distressing to everyone – including the person who makes the mistake in the first place.

Reference codes

You may be asked to add a reference code to any document you are preparing and in any software – although these are more commonly used in databases.

A reference code is simply an abbreviated method of saying something. For example:

- In every catalogue you will see an 'item code'. This is a reference code for the supplier.
- If you work then you will have a tax code. This is a reference code for the Inland Revenue and for your salary section.
- If you are a student then you will have a student reference (or ID) number. This is a reference code used by your college.
- Wherever you live, you will have a postcode. This is a reference code for the Royal Mail and other mail handling organisations.

Reference codes are used because they provide a lot of information in a limited number of characters. There is therefore a 'key' which translates them. For instance, a student ID may be as follows:

280784JakesL01

In this case, 280784 is the student's date of birth (28 July 1984), the last name is Jakes and the initial of the first name is L. The number 01 is allocated in case another L Jakes with the same birthdate is enrolled. This student would then be 280784JakesL02.

The idea of a reference code is to make each separate item **unique**. This provides a very quick way of finding records.

If you are asked to add a reference code *always:*

- make sure you know how these are assigned – so you understand the system
- *check* if you think the reference code is unusual in any way or if you believe it doesn't match your system
- think carefully if you have to assign any yourself.

1 It is useful to know how the Inland Revenue tax code system works – then you can understand yours!

- The tax code is made up of a number and then a letter.
- The number is used to work out how much tax you must pay.
- The letter indicates your personal status. It does not affect how much you pay, but shows how you may be affected by any tax changes announced in the Budget. Most people under 65 are coded L.
- The amount of allowances you are allowed are added together (e.g. your personal allowance).
- The amount of any deductions you are allowed are added together (e.g. a union subscription payment).
- The deductions are subtracted from the allowances to give the tax-free amount for the year. Above this figure you pay tax.
- The tax code is the tax-free amount with the last figure removed.

For example, Jocelyn Fisher has personal allowances which total £4585. Her deductions are £382. Her tax free pay is therefore £4203. Her tax code would therefore be 420L.

If you are working, check your own tax code and see if you can understand it better.

2 If you are a driver, look at your driving licence and find one example of a code. Then see if you can find out how this has been created!

Test your knowledge and understanding

1 **a** If you enrolled at a college which used a reference code system similar to that described on page 168, and you were the first student of your name to enrol, can you work out your reference code?

   b If you are a college student and have a reference code or ID code, find out how this works and why you were allocated that particular code.

2 An employee has a personal allowance of £4385 in 2001/2. She has no deductions. What will her tax code be assuming she is categorised as 'L'?

3 Look back at the spreadsheet illustration on page 157. Can you find any examples of reference codes? Can you guess how they may have been devised?

Deleting or amending data

You may be asked to delete data which has been previously entered or amend data – in which case you will delete it and then replace it.

In both these cases it is easier if you can move straight to the data you need to delete and amend. This is much better than hunting for it – especially in a very long document (or in a very large database). Element 105.2 explains how to do this.

Evidence collection

Start a collection of print-outs showing the data you have input into a computer. Note that this must include both words and numbers.

If you add reference codes then identify these on your print-outs.

You also need to prove that you can delete or amend existing data *and* identify and correct your own mistakes. The easiest way to prove this is to take a print out *before* you have made any deletions, amendments or corrections and then take another one afterwards. Then highlight the changes you made and fasten the sheets together.

Note that if you do not enter or search by reference codes, your assessor may want to check that you understand why these are sometimes used.

Element 105.2 | Find data on a computer

You will frequently have to find data on a computer. This may be because you have been asked to find it and say what it is, or because you need to take a print-out, or because you need to find it before you amend or delete it.

Searching for data

One obvious way to search for data on any software package you use is to bring up on screen the document you need and then browse through it to find what you need. But usually there are quicker ways of finding what you need.

Finding data on a Microsoft package

The easiest way is to use your search facility. You will find this under Edit on your Menu bar. Click Edit and then scroll down to Find. You will then see your Find and Replace dialogue box.

● If you just want to find some data, type the key data you need to find into the 'Find what' box and then click Find Next. This will move to the first occurrence of the word or number you have entered – but you can then decide what to do.

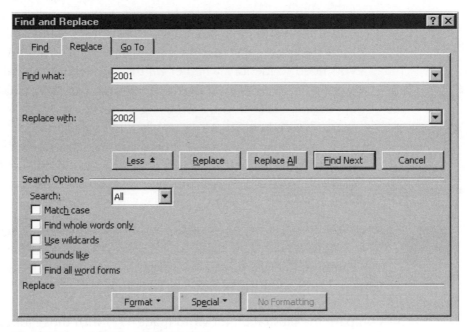

Word Find and Replace dialogue box

In Word, if you click on the 'More' box you can refine your search. For instance you can choose:

– match case
– whole word only
– use wild cards.

These are the most common options. For instance, you want to find 'March' but not 'march'. Match case means that upper and lower case letters will be matched – so if you type March and click this box, you will only find the month of March, not the verb 'to march'.

If you want to find the word 'car' but don't want words which contain the syllable 'car' – such as card or placard – you can click the whole word to restrict your search to 'car'.

Finally, if you can remember part of a word but not all, you can use a wild card. For instance, you want to find the name of a customer. You can't remember if she is called Darwin or Dawson. You could type Da* and then click wild card. This will find all the names starting with Da and then containing other characters.

You can also combine boxes (by ticking more than one) – to restrict your searches even further. The more you restrict them, the quicker you are likely to find what you want.

- If you want to amend some data, which is consistent throughout your document, then you can use Find and Replace. As an example, in a table you have been told to put 20% in a column and are now told this should have been 25%. You can use Find and Replace to both find *and* substitute the new data automatically. At this point, you need to identify whether *all* the occurrences should be replaced automatically or only some of them. You can then make the appropriate selection by choosing either Replace (to replace the first occurrence); Replace All (to replace every occurrence) or Find Next. As a basic rule of thumb – unless you are absolutely certain – always select Find Next and then you have the option of deciding what to do each time.

Check it out

The Find and Replace facility varies slightly, depending upon the software you are using – but the principle is the same.

Compare the illustration for Word (page 171) with those for Excel and Access below. Then make sure you know how to operate Find and Replace on the software you use regularly.

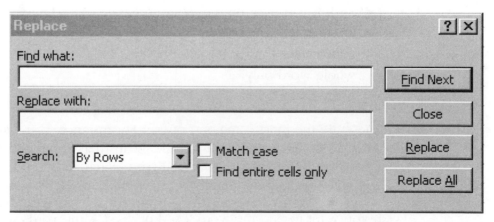

Excel Find and Replace dialogue box

Access Find and Replace dialogue box

Searching in a database

In addition to using your Find facility, a database designer may have included other search facilities to help you. In this case you can enter a key word and search on this. Or an index may have been designed as part of your database and you can either scroll down this or search for a key word.

In all databases, too, a unique reference code or item of key data is allocated to a **key field**. As you saw on page 148, this is a special field which contains a specific item of data which is unique to that record. For instance:

- on a student record, the student ID would be in the key field
- on a bank account, the account number would be in the key field
- on a staff record, the payroll number would be in the key field.

If you know this item of data you can go straight to the record. It is when you do not know it that search facilities are so essential!

Developing your skills

As you progress your IT skills you will learn other methods of searching. These include Sorting data (e.g. moving it into a different order) or Filtering data to find *exactly* what you want. You can do this in both database and spreadsheet packages.

Print routines

Frequently you will be asked to produce a hard (paper) copy of a document, worksheet or database record. You do this by taking a print-out.

On Windows software, you select print from your File menu *or* you can click on the small printer icon on your toolbar. However, it is important that you know how to make certain checks before you start:

- **Always** check whether you should print:
  - the whole document
  - selected pages from a document
  - the current page
  - selected text from a document.

  This will alter the selection you make on the print dialogue box.
- If you have any concerns whether the document will look acceptable on paper, go to File then Print Preview to view it on screen first.
- If you need to make any changes to the size of paper or whether the document is printed down the page (portrait) or across a page (landscape), then you do this by accessing File and then Page Setup.
- If you have been asked to take a number of copies, take one first and check it is satisfactory before taking the remainder.

Check it out!

1   Find a document you prepared recently and then print out:
   - just one page
   - selected text
   - one or two selected pages.

2   Develop your skills. Type out a short document of one or two paragraphs. Then alter your print options so that you print it out across a sheet of A4 paper (i.e. landscape) instead of down the paper (i.e. portrait). It will obviously look better if you change the margins so the page is much wider – ask your tutor or supervisor for guidance if you don't know how to do this.

Providing the data

Remember that whether you have been asked to provide information on the data you read on screen, or a print-out, you should make sure that this is only given to authorised people.

The easy way, if you are not sure whether you can give information to someone, is simply to make a note of their request but say you don't have the data to hand at present. Then check with your supervisor or team leader if it is acceptable to pass on the information to that person.

Finally, if you keep a copy of print-outs yourself, do make sure you store these safely and put them away after use, preferably in a locked filing cabinet. Leaving papers strewn all over the desk means the data is available for everyone to see.

Evidence collection

You need to prove that you can find both words and numbers on your software using *both*:

- automatic searching using key data
- manual browsing through the data on your computer.

You can do this either by demonstrating how you search for words and numbers on your system to your assessor *or* keeping a record of the searches you have made. It would be useful if you state why you have made these and what changes were required. If you do Find and Replace in any document, for instance, take a copy both before and after you have done this operation, to prove what you have done.

Contribute to maintaining customer service

> This unit is one of two Optional Group B units. You need to do *either* this unit *or* unit 107 to gain your award, but not both.

This unit is concerned with the way:

- you communicate with customers for whom you provide a service
- in which you provide services to customers.

It is **important** because:

- every organisation needs external customers to survive in business
- external customers will go elsewhere if they are unhappy with the service they receive
- you may deal with external customers as part of your job
- you will also have your own 'internal' customers – who themselves deal with external customers.

This unit comprises two elements. Before you start, you need to understand why customer service is so important and how this will affect your own job as an administrator.

Key skills signpost

If you are studying your key skills award in Communication at level 1 then you can extend your customer service skills and obtain evidence for your key skills portfolio through your work for this unit.

Special note: You will need to do activity C2.2 *before* you do C2.1a or C1.2b.

C2.1a   In a small group of 3 or 4, discuss occasions when you have been satisfied with customer service you have received and occasions when you have been dissatisfied. Contribute to the discussion from the ideas you have noted as part of your work for C2.2. The aim is to reach agreement on the five features of customer service your group considers the most important.

C2.1b   Discuss with your tutor the importance of body language when you are communicating with customers face-to-face. In particular, identify the type of gestures, postures and facial expressions which people use in specific situations, such as when they are impatient, annoyed or very nervous. Explain how understanding these can help you to deal with customers more effectively. Use the ideas you have noted as part of your work for C2.2 to help you.

After you have completed each of your discussions, write a brief summary about how the notes you made helped you in each case.

C2.2   Check through the content of this unit in this book and make notes which you think will help you in your discussions for C2.1a. You can, of course, research additional information on customer service, or use a different book, to supplement your own ideas.

Obtain one book from your College or local library which gives you information about body language. Select a book which has clear illustrations.

Read this carefully and make a note of the key points which you think will help you in your discussions for C2.1b. Remember – you are trying to find out about body language in relation to customers. However, you will find that body language books also contain other interesting information – such as how to see if someone likes you when they meet you!

If you prefer, you could surf the net instead. Try www.ask.co.uk and type 'non-verbal communication' as your question. Then see what you can find!

C2.3   **a**   You work for South Winds insurance company. An external customer, Mrs Sheila Morris, called in to see your boss, Bill Evans, yesterday. Unfortunately Bill was out at the time. Mrs Morris told you that her son, Tim, is going to university in September and she wanted to know if her household insurance policy would cover his personal possessions (such as his stereo and computer) if he takes them with him. You couldn't help her but said you would find out and let her know.

You have now established that his possessions will be covered up to a total value of £1,500 on her existing policy.

Write a letter to send to Mrs Morris at her home address – 48 Weighbridge Road, Hightown, HG5 3EL – giving her this information and asking her to contact your boss if she thinks the value will be above this amount.

b   Investigate customer service at three or four places where *you* are a regular customer. Instead of simply shopping, or calling in, find a reason to ask a question and then assess how promptly you are dealt with and the manner and attitude of the staff.

After you have completed your investigations, write a short report on your experiences and say how customer service could be improved if you found it to be poor . Your report must include *one* image. This could be a picture, chart, sketch or diagram. For instance, if you have decided on a method of 'scoring' each place, you may want to put a table into your report which shows your results.

Contribute to maintaining customer service

What is customer service? The term is used to describe the way in which staff in an organisation deal with customers – their attitude, the speed of their response, the help they provide and whether they will make an extra effort to make sure the customer is satisfied after the encounter. Because customers are so important they are the responsibility of everyone in an organisation.

If you have some experience in this area, you can obviously apply this in an administrative job and it may also help you to obtain additional evidence towards this unit.

Why effective customer service is important

You are a customer yourself. You visit numerous suppliers of goods and services every week and expect to receive good service. But how do customers actually evaluate the service they receive?

Assume a new pizza restaurant has opened in your area. You decide to go with a friend to try it out. It's light and airy and very modern. The menu looks good and the prices are reasonable. When your pizza arrives it's hot and freshly cooked. You might be happy to become a regular customer.

But what if you had been kept waiting for 10 minutes before anyone asked what you wanted? When the waiter arrived he was surly and unpleasant and then muddled up your order. Then you had to wait over 30 minutes before your food arrived. When you tried to ask for another drink you couldn't get anyone's attention and there was a queue of people waiting to come in.

Finally, the waiter rushed to your table, gave you the bill and asked you to pay quickly so they can have your table for someone else. How happy would you be to go back now?

As you can see, a good product can be ruined by poor customer service.

Information update

Studies have shown that it costs five times as much to attract a new customer as to keep an existing customer. It has also been proved that if customers have a good experience they may tell one or two people about it, but if customers have a bad experience they will tell about eight other people how awful something is. So word spreads quickly!

External and internal customers

In a restaurant you are an external customer. However, as an administrator you are likely to have both external *and* internal customers.

External customers are easy to understand. These are all the other businesses or private individuals who contact or visit your organisation because they want to buy your product or service.

Internal customers are people who work in your organisation but who want you to provide a service for them. A typical example is someone from another department who asks for some information or who needs a copy of a document you have in your filing system. Normally you don't count members of your own team as your customers – just other people *outside* your team.

You must support internal customers in order to give good service to external customers

Both these types of customers are important. In every transaction *someone* is trying to provide a service for an external customer. You may be part of that process, even if you are not dealing with the external customer direct. If you let down your internal customer, he or he cannot provide a good service to the external customer.

Identifying your customers

Your external customers may be business organisations, private individuals or both. In a small firm, your internal customers may work in another section or office. In a large organisation, they will probably work in a different department altogether.

Knowing who your customers are helps you to understand what they are likely to need. If you know this, you can make sure you have the information you need to help them promptly with routine queries and requests.

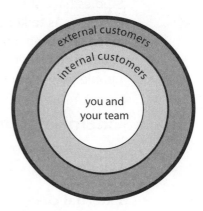

Do you know who your customers are?

Test your knowledge and understanding

Each of the four administrators below deals with customers.

a From the description of their job role, can you state which ones deal with:

  i both external and internal customers, and
  ii only internal customers?

b If the administrator is not responsible for dealing with the external customers, can you say who is?

  1 Tahira works in a sales office. She prepares and logs all the sales visits made by representatives. The sales reps often contact her if they have an urgent query.

  2 Sue works in a large college. She works in the student services area and assists the Student Services Manager. Everyone in this section is trained to help any students who call in with an enquiry.

  3 Martin also works in the college – in the finance section. He logs invoices into the computer system. If there is a query from a supplier about payment, this is dealt with by Maria, his team leader, who may need information from him.

4   Paula is an administrator for a team of web page designers who work for a small firm. She liaises with other teams when she needs specialist information or if they need information from her. She also answers the telephone and deals with general enquiries.

Evidence collection

For any situation in which you have provided a service or worked as an administrator, identify:

- the people who were your customers
- whether they were internal, external or both
- if they were internal, the person who dealt with the external customers.

Note that this could be in a part-time job, on work experience or when you were working in a college office or training office.

Keep this information safely. You will be adding to it later in this unit.

Passing on queries and complaints

To do your job properly you need to know how to answer routine queries or to provide basic information. You also need to know how to respond if you are asked for information you don't have or don't know.

- Sonia is not confident. If someone asks her something she often dithers. A typical Sonia answer may be, 'Oh goodness, I've no idea. Sorry. Can you ask someone else?'

- Sean is the opposite and is apt to be over-confident. He likes to pretend he knows the answers even if he doesn't. Yesterday he told a customer some goods would definitely be delivered tomorrow – even though he hadn't checked the delivery list.

- Fatima, on the other hand, tries to help but is decisive and honest when she cannot. Her standard response in this situation is, 'I'm sorry, I don't have that information available. Can you leave it with me and I'll find out and call you back as soon as possible?'

   Fatima then finds out the information. If the query is complex or relates to a different area then she makes sure the person who can handle the query knows what is needed and leaves it to them. If, however, the information is straightforward she also makes a note of it so that she will know the answer herself next time.

Fatima also knows that complaints must be passed on to her team leader immediately, because dealing with these is not part of her job role.

SONIA
(nice but timid)

SEAN
(confident but not competent)

FATIMA
(friendly and efficient)

Who would you prefer to work with?

Test your knowledge and understanding

1   If you were a customer and regularly dealt with Sonia, what do you think your reaction would be – and why?

2   Sean thinks he is wonderful with customers. Do you agree? Can you think of any consequences of Sean's methods of dealing with people?

3   Why is it important that you learn how to deal with routine queries yourself?

4   **a**   Can you suggest *two* examples of a routine query which many administrators may have to deal with?

    b   From your suggestions, what type of information do you think administrators need close to hand?

(**Note** If you are doing this question as a group, pool your ideas and compare your suggestions with other people's.)

Customers with special needs

Not all customers are the same. Your customers – both internal and external – may include people with special needs, including a wide range of disabilities or impairments, for instance:

- those who are hard of hearing or deaf
- those who have a visual impairment or who are blind
- those who have mobility problems and need to use a stick, walking frame or wheelchair.

Today most organisations are both sensitive and alert to providing appropriate facilities for disabled customers and staff – such as ramps for wheelchairs and wider doors, disabled toilet facilities, braille buttons in lifts and so on.

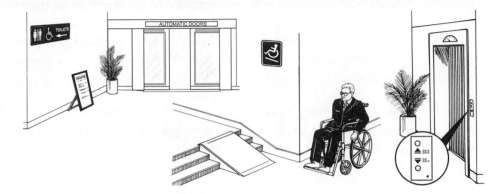

You need to know what facilities exist in your organisation so that you can provide this information to your customers. You also need to inform your team leader if you think that a particular facility is lacking and would be useful. However, on their own these facilities will soon be forgotten if the attitude of staff is all wrong.

The golden rules you should follow are summarised in the chart below.

Dealing with customers with special needs	
Do	**Don't**
• Speak more slowly and enunciate your words properly if someone has a hearing impairment so they can lip read more easily. Offer to provide a leaflet or write down important points for them.	• Be frightened about dealing with people who are different from yourself.
• Remember people with a visual impairment often have acute hearing! They will also listen attentively. Offer to read out a form or point to a line on which they need to sign their name. Ideally your firm should provide customer materials in large print as an option – if not, suggest it.	• Confuse a physical disability with a mental one and treat people as dim because they cannot see, hear or walk as well as you can!
	• Treat disabled people as 'odd' or 'different' in any way.
	• Pretend the disability doesn't exist (or stare at it fixedly!)
	• Shout if you can tell the person is slightly deaf.
• Move from behind a high counter if someone is in a wheelchair and can't see you properly. Offer to open doors for them, unless these are automatic.	• Be embarrassed if someone says they cannot see very well.

If you know someone who has a disability ask them what they think of standards of customer service in organisations they visit – and their views on the facilities provided. Try to draw up a list of good points that please them and attitudes and actions that drive them mad! You might get a few surprises!

Alternatively, one day, when you leave home, imagine you are in a wheelchair. Then think about how you would cope with all the situations you meet from that moment until you arrive at your desk.

The limits of your job role

Sean was an obvious example of an administrator who exceeded his job role. When you are dealing with customers:

- never guess the answer
- never make promises you can't keep
- never make promises someone else would have to keep without their authorisation.

You are likely to be expected to deal with most routine enquiries yourself. However, if a query relates to another area or is complex, always ask for guidance.

Similarly, you may be expected to deal with basic complaints and record these but should not suggest any solutions unless you are absolutely certain this is a standard answer in this situation. Normally you should make a note of the complaint and refer it to your team leader.

Finally, do check the type of customers you are expected to deal with direct and those who you are not. For example, if your boss regularly deals with Joanna White, and asks you to find out some information for her, he may be a bit surprised if you announce you rang her yourself with it this morning. Similarly, if your team leader asks you to obtain some information for a senior manager in another department, it's unlikely you will be expected to pass it on yourself unless you have been told to do so.

Communicate with customers

The better your communication skills are, the more likely you are to provide an excellent service. 'Communication' includes:

- talking face-to-face
- talking on the telephone
- learning how to listen
- projecting the right body language.

Talking face-to-face

You may talk to external customers face-to-face. You will certainly talk to your internal customers face-to-face quite regularly. Communicating face-to-face was first covered in Unit 101, page 31. In relation to customers, you should note the following.

- Greet people with a smile (or a smile in your voice). Look cheerful!
- Don't keep people waiting. If this is unavoidable, acknowledge their presence and arrange to get help. Then tell them what you've done.
- If there is any type of delay, keep people informed.
- Ask the customer what you can do to help them.
- Listen carefully to the response.
- Use 'reflective' body language to show you are really listening and understanding them – such as nodding, leaning towards them, looking at them properly, looking sympathetic if they have a problem.
- If you can't help the customer yourself, find someone who can.
- Be positive. '*Never say never*' is a useful slogan. 'I'll see what I can do,' is positive. 'We can't do that' is not.
- Be prepared to make the extra effort, for example to show a customer where something is, to track down a particular piece of information or to help someone fill in a form they are finding difficult.

On the telephone

Again this was covered in Unit 101, page 33. Remember, if you are pleasant and helpful to everyone, then people will be pleased they have spoken to you.

Check it out!

Turn back to Unit 101, pages 31–36 and refresh your memory about communicating with people both face-to-face and over the telephone.

Then decide whether it is good, or bad, customer service to hold callers in a queue because the lines are busy (or play 'music on hold') – and how this may affect the attitude of customers you speak to. If you are studying in a group, discuss your own experiences and compare your views.

Information update

Surveys on customer service have shown that using a little bit of psychology often comes in useful. This means thinking about how people react to situations and acting accordingly.

As an example, people who are delayed become impatient. If you explain to a customer (internal or external) that there will be a delay before someone can see them or before some work can be completed, they will expect you to give an estimate of how long they will have to wait. If you say 10 minutes – but then have to apologise again and say it will be another 10 minutes, this is extremely irritating. If, however, you say 15 minutes and then the delay is only 10 minutes they are often both relieved and pleased.

If there is a delay try to keep people informed

The secret, therefore, is always to slightly *over-estimate* a delay and then try to deliver early, rather than *under-estimate* a delay and have to disappoint people again!

Projecting a positive image

When you are a customer, you can have a variety of different reactions to an encounter with someone trying to provide a service:

- you remember them with pleasure as being helpful and efficient
- you have no particular memory of them
- you remember them as being actively annoying or even useless.

Do you project a positive image to your customers?

In the first case the person has projected a positive image. In the second the image is 'neutral' – or even non-existent. In the third case you have received a negative image.

Always remember

- A good first impression is vital. You never get the opportunity to do this twice. As a first step, when a customer approaches you:
  - stop what you are doing and give them your full attention
  - look at them when you are talking to them
  - remember that a smile costs nothing, and even works over the telephone!
- To the external customer you represent your firm. In fact, you 'are' the firm to them at that moment.
- External customers cost a lot to obtain in advertising and promotion. Yet you have the power to lose or annoy a customer in two minutes' flat.

- A positive image depends upon:
  - your appearance – if you look smart and tidy it projects an image of efficiency to the customers you meet
  - your voice – speak clearly and don't shout!
  - your expression, which should be of interest or concern not irritation
  - the words you use, which should be appropriate to the situation, and
  - your attitude, which shows you realise how important each customer is.

All these must give the same message at the same time! The message should be 'You are my customer, you are important to me, I have time for you and want to meet your needs.'

Test your knowledge and understanding

Always giving a positive image is very difficult. It is easy when you have plenty of time, the customer is pleasant or someone you like and their request is reasonable and straightforward. It is much harder on a bad day, when the customer is Tim from Finance who you find difficult to talk to and when you can't understand what he wants!

1 **a** Identify at least two occasions when you know you have been less than pleased to be interrupted by a customer.
   b How does this show – by your voice, expression, attitude?
   c How do you think this makes the customer feel?

2 **a** Identify at least four types of customers – or customer situations – you find difficult to deal with.
   b Suggest how you could be better prepared to cope with them.

3 If you are having difficulties understanding a customer, what would you do? Discuss your ideas with your tutor or supervisor. Keep your suggestions safely and check them with the information you will read on page 192.

Dealing with customers politely and promptly

All organisations set standards for dealing with customers. Some standards are more rigorous than others. In some organisations, for instance, there may be:

- a corporate uniform
- a time limit by when visitors must be seen
- a time limit by when phone calls must be answered (e.g. within four rings)
- a standard response for staff greeting external customers, either over the telephone or face-to-face. Often this involves giving your name, e.g. 'Hello, Software Unlimited, Martine speaking. How can I help you?'

In many administrative jobs, however, you will find you have rather more flexibility. In this case, it will be taken for granted that you will always be polite to your customers and deal with them promptly. This should apply to both your internal and external customers. Remember, your customers will normally be busy people themselves, who have their own deadlines and standards to meet. They need your help to achieve them!

Communicating clearly and confidently

You have already seen how important this is. It actually helps if you know you have to give a standard greeting because then you have a 'script' which can help you feel more confident.

Clear communication

This depends upon your ability to:

- speak clearly
- listen carefully
- say what you mean
- be courteous.

These are worth looking at separately.

Speaking clearly This sounds simple – but it is amazing how many people mutter, or look anywhere but at the person they are speaking to! This makes it far more difficult to understand someone. *Always* make eye contact with the person to whom you are speaking. The *pace* at which you speak is also important. Unfortunately, if you are nervous, you may be tempted to gabble, which makes matters even worse.

Listen carefully Very few people are good listeners! Most of us want the other person to finish quickly, then we can say what we have just thought of – so we are not listening properly. Try to develop your listening skills so that you can repeat back what someone has said to you a few minutes later.

Say what you mean This means choosing the correct words and being precise. Refer to people properly by name and, if necessary, by job title so it is clear who you mean. Speak in proper sentences – so that you respond in a conversation. Don't use slang and remember that if you say 'OK' this will probably be taken as an agreement that you have understood and will do something – so don't say 'OK' just to confirm you have heard someone!

Be courteous In other words, speak politely. If you say something which someone finds rude or insulting then this will act as a 'communication barrier' between you – as the other person is likely to be annoyed. These are some useful tips.

- If you don't know whether you can call someone by their first name or not, use their formal title. They will quickly tell you if they would like you to be more informal.

- Expect to be more formal with senior staff at work and with external customers – especially those who are older than you.

- Be wary of being tactless and think before you speak.

- Try to avoid asking personal questions, such as 'How old are you?' If you must obtain personal information from a customer as part of your job, phrase it diplomatically, e.g. 'Would you mind telling me your age – I need it for your application form.' Often just saying *why* you need the information makes all the difference!

Communicating confidently

Your confidence will increase if you:

- develop your communication skills
- learn as much as you can about your job and the work of other members of your team.

This is because you will have the answers you need at your fingertips more easily. Until you reach this stage, it is useful if you know who *can* help you if you are faced with a query you cannot answer yourself, because you can respond appropriately without hesitation.

Giving information and answering queries

It is useful if you keep information which people often request close at hand. This is why every reception desk or customer service area has a variety of booklets, leaflets and forms available for external customers. In relation to internal customers, this may mean having to obtain files or other documents quickly which will give you the correct information.

You also need to know the type of information you are allowed to give to people – and the queries you are allowed to answer – and those which you must refer to other people.

Information should be close at hand and organised neatly

If ever you are in any doubt about this, *always* refer a request or query to someone else rather than take a risk. It is too late to find out later that the information was confidential!

However, even if you know your job very well indeed *and* know the limits of your authority, there will still be occasions when:

- you are asked for information you haven't got (or cannot find)
- you are asked a query you don't understand (or cannot answer)
- a customer is making a serious complaint and you are out of your depth (see page 201).

The secret is not to panic but to do something positive instead.

If the customer is on the telephone

- Explain that you don't keep that particular item of information but will find it and send it to them – then do just that.
- If the query is urgent or the complaint is serious, ask a member of your team for assistance.
- If you are on your own, take down all the details and reassure the customer you will pass them on immediately and arrange for someone to call them back quickly.

If the customer is with you

- Find out exactly what information they want and see if you can send it by post or phone them later. Or ask them to wait a moment and ask a team member for assistance.

● Again, if the query is urgent or the complaint is serious, ask someone for assistance – even if this means having to ask the customer to wait for a short time until you find someone.

Communication problems

You may experience communication problems for one of three reasons:

● you cannot understand your customer
● your customer cannot understand you
● the customer is upset, agitated or annoyed and this is forming a 'barrier' between you.

Understanding your customer

You may have problems understanding customers who:

● don't speak English very well, such as foreign visitors
● have a speech impairment
● have a very strong accent
● are talking in technical terms or jargon you don't understand.

Foreign visitors If you have ever learned a foreign language and tried to speak it abroad you will know how difficult it can be to cope with a rapid, fluent reply! To this customer *you* are the person speaking the foreign language. It will therefore help if you:

● speak relatively slowly and *very* clearly (separate your words)
● use simple English words
● use short sentences
● avoid slang expressions they won't understand
● try to rephrase your sentence if you think they haven't understood you
● listen carefully when they repeat something back to you to check they really have understood you
● write down and give them dates and numbers they need to know.

Sometimes you may experience communication problems

Customers with a speech impairment could include someone who is profoundly deaf, or even someone who has just had a number of teeth removed at a local dentist! In this situation:

- concentrate on what is being said to you
- listen carefully
- repeat back what you have heard to check you are both understanding each other
- try to be understanding rather than embarrassed
- *never* confuse a speech impairment with a lack of intelligence.

Customers with a very strong accent may be foreigners or people from one of the regions of Britain where there is a strong local dialect. In this case:

- again concentrate on what is being said
- ask the customer to speak more slowly or repeat what they are saying
- repeat back what you have heard to check you have understood them correctly.

Customers speaking in technical terms or jargon are more likely to be your internal customers than your external customers. There will be an assumption you know what they are talking about and have heard the expressions or abbreviations they are using before. This is mainly likely to happen when you first start a new job. You should therefore:

- explain that you are not a technical expert or have not heard the term they are using – *never* pretend you know something you don't!
- write down the word or abbreviation and read it back to them
- ask a team member for help if you can't cope
- then ask the same team member to explain what it was all about afterwards – that's how you learn!

Your customer cannot understand you

If you genuinely feel you have done everything you can to communicate with a customer, ask for assistance before the experience becomes an ordeal – for both of you.

Feelings as a barrier

A typical barrier to communication is strong feelings. If you are very upset, excited or angry then you don't communicate in the same way you do normally. Neither do your customers.

You can usually tell how a customer is feeling by the way they start a conversation:

- a nervous person may speak very hesitantly and not look at you properly
- an excited person will speak quickly

- someone who is upset may find it very difficult to say how they feel
- an angry person will want to say how they feel immediately and explain what is annoying them.

Nervous people can be helped if you smile, take your time and do not rush them.

Excited people may have to be asked to slow down if they are speaking too quickly. Often it is better to let them say what they want – and then start again!

Upset people may not even be able to have a proper conversation with you until they have calmed down. If there is genuine distress then try to arrange for the customer to sit down in a private office and immediately notify one of your team members.

Angry people need to be allowed to say what is annoying them. Therefore:

- *don't* interrupt
- apologise for the problem on behalf of your team (this isn't the same as accepting the blame!)
- note down all the details
- assure the customer you will refer the problem to someone to deal with straightaway – and do so
- try not to get upset. Treat it as an issue rather than a personal attack. However, this doesn't mean you have to accept any verbal abuse. In this situation, ask your team leader for help immediately.

Evidence collection

1   On page 181 you listed the type of customers you normally deal with. Now write a brief description of your own job role. Explain why you regularly deal with customers and the type of queries or information you have to give. Make sure you include a brief description of the type of queries you must refer to other people because they are not part of your job.

2   You now need to keep a record of the communications you have with them. For *each* customer – or type of customer – you have listed, identify:

   a   the ways in which you normally communicate with them
   b   the main reason for the communication.

   You must provide evidence for your assessor that you communicate:

   - both face-to-face *and* on the telephone
   - with both internal and external customers.

   It is therefore sensible to check your record to make sure that you have included all these requirements and to keep it safe until you can do this.

3 If you have any problems communicating with customers write a short note about this. State what happened and what you did. Bear in mind this is not saying the problem was your fault. The customer may have been very angry or may not speak English very well. You must explain how you coped in this situation. If this doesn't occur, you can expect your assessor to discuss with you what you would do if it did!

4 Ask your line manager, team leader or supervisor for witness testimony to say that you regularly communicate with customers clearly, that you deal with people politely and promptly and that you refer any problems to someone promptly.

5 Write a brief account explaining how you try to present a positive image of yourself to customers and say why this is important. Ask your line manager, team leader or supervisor to countersign this for you.

Element 106.2   Provide services to customers

As an administrator, your customer services will often relate to providing services to people. For instance, your external customers may need information or a message passing on to someone; your internal customers may want you to do something for them.

The type of services you provide

Some teams are mainly responsible for dealing with external customers – but need the support of other people in the organisation to do this. A typical example is a sales team.

Other teams mainly deal with internal customers and provide information, a variety of services or both. An example would be a centralised reprographics unit which does photocopying for all the staff.

Another type of team deals with both external and internal customers. A good example is human resources or personnel which deals with job applicants or people enquiring about vacancies *and* with staff who want information or advice.

A human resources team deals with internal and external customers

If you work in a general office, you may be asked to undertake a range of services for a variety of internal customers, such as:

- typing a document
- retrieving a document from the files
- photocopying a document
- returning a file to a cabinet.

You need to establish:

- what type of services your team provides to external customers
- what type of services your team provides to internal customers
- how these services 'fit' into the services offered by the organisation as a whole.

Being clear about what the customer requires

There are normally three stages to identifying a customer's requirements.

1   Find out who you are talking to, if you don't already know. Ask politely, e.g. 'Could you give me your name, please' or 'Could you tell me who's calling please' – *not* 'Who are you?'

2   Find out what the customer wants. This is easy if your customer knows! 'How can I help you?' or 'What can I do for you?' is better than 'Yes?' or 'What do you want?'

Listen to the response and remember that it is better to write down the specific request (see next page).

3   If your customer doesn't know exactly what he or she wants then you need to ask questions to find out. For example:

- identify what facts you need to know to be able to help
- start difficult (or repeat) questions with 'I'm sorry but . . .' e.g. 'I'm sorry but could you repeat that?' or 'I'm sorry, but who did you deal with before?'
- *listen* to the replies
- use your common sense – the more you know your job, the organisation and your own work area the easier it is to hazard an accurate guess as to what the customer really wants or needs
- if you are still struggling, ask the customer to wait a moment and get someone else to help you.

Whatever the customer requires, you need to make sure you know *exactly* what you are being asked to do and how quickly the service is required. It is therefore extremely important that you find out key facts. These usually include:

- what is required
- the size of the task
- any relevant deadlines.

There is a big difference between being asked to type a 10-page document in an hour and being asked to put a folder away when you have time!

It is always important to find out the deadline first

The importance of agreeing and keeping a note of a customer's requirements

It is important that you know the type of requests to which you are expected to agree immediately and those which you should refer to someone else. Generally, you will be expected to agree immediately if the request is:

- made by a senior member of staff
- for a routine service provided by your team.

However, do be careful not to commit your team to a deadline without agreement from your team leader! Simply say that you have to refer the request to your boss and will confirm the details later.

It will help other members of your team if you make a clear note of the request. This can either be a short note or – in some cases – may be recorded on a special form (see below). Always make sure you have all the key facts and details your team leader will need to make a decision and pass on the request promptly.

Test your knowledge and understanding

1 Read the paragraph at the top of page 199 and then decide which of the following jobs you would agree to do and which you would not. Give a reason for each answer and say *how* you would turn down each request. Check your suggestions with your supervisor or tutor.

   a An external customer asks for a team member's home telephone number.

   b A senior manager asks you to photocopy two pages of a report for him because he needs it urgently.

   c A sales rep, who is supposed to produce his own reports, asks if you will type up a 6-page document he has written because his handwriting is so poor.

   d The PA (personal assistant) to a senior manager phones asking you for the names and addresses of two customers from the files.

   e Your office stationery supplier telephones, asking if you can send a copy of your recent order by fax, because they have lost the original.

   f A customer phones for your latest catalogue and price list.

2 Maria works in a reprographics section. She is tired of receiving requests for photocopying she cannot understand and has decided to prepare a form for requests. She has received the following suggestions:

   - name of person making request
   - department
   - internal telephone extension
   - date of request
   - date by which the photocopies are required
   - number of original documents
   - number of copies required
   - whether stapled or not
   - whether back-to-back or not.

   Beneath the form, she wants a short section to be completed by reprographics staff to say when the item was photocopied and by whom.

   a From the information given, draft a form to issue to her customers.

   b Identify *two* benefits to Maria and her team of issuing this form.

   c Identify *two* benefits to her customers.

   Check your suggestions with your supervisor or tutor.

The services you cannot provide

In most cases you will be expected to agree to a request, but there are certain occasions when this may be difficult or impossible. The time to hesitate is if:

- the task is too difficult for you
- the task relates to work not normally undertaken by your team
- the person asking is someone for whom your team doesn't normally do work
- you have been personally asked to do the work but this would mean you couldn't do other urgent tasks you have promised to do
- there is a problem being experienced by your team and your team leader has given explicit instructions that any new work cannot be done just yet
- you are being asked for confidential information.

This doesn't mean you just say 'No!' It means that you say to your customer that you will have to check with your supervisor or team leader first – and you do just that.

Making sure information is accurate and up-to-date

You will stand a better chance of making sure your information is accurate and up-to-date if you have neat and tidy files and if you regularly throw away old or outdated documents! As a typical example, a catalogue may be produced to last for a year, because it is expensive, but there may be three updates to a separate price list in this time. Throwing away the old one whenever you receive a new one is vital in this situation. The same applies if you receive updated leaflets or brochures on your services or products.

Many organisations insert a special footer at the bottom of printed pages to help you. For instance, it may say 'v2.23.6.02'. This means that you are looking at version two, produced on the 23 June 2002. If you then see 'v3.14.11.02' in the file as well, you should check first, but it is fairly safe to say that version 2 has now had its day!

Information which is more difficult to check relates to:

- current events relating to customers or internal matters
- staff movements and opinions.

If you access a customer file you are trusting that the document on top is the last one to be received, but this may not be true. Another document (or more) may have been received and not yet have been placed in the file.

You also cannot guess the situation in relation to internal issues. If your Safety Officer rings to ask if your boss has done anything about a particular matter you will not know – unless you ask.

Staff movements relate to staff who have left, new staff who have arrived, staff holiday leave and staff who are off ill.

Finally, you can never guess what your team members or team leader is thinking unless you are told. The enquiry 'Do you know if John intends to go to Belgium next week?' must be answered with 'No, I'm sorry, but I'll find out and let you know' – unless John has already told you.

The safe way is to say you are not certain unless you are *sure*. Then always check before you give a response.

The importance of providing a service within agreed timescales

Once you have agreed to perform an administrative support service by a certain time, it is your responsibility to do this. If you are having problems, then do make sure you notify either your team leader or the person who asked you to do the work promptly and clearly explain *why* you are having difficulties.

Checking customer satisfaction

Checking customer satisfaction is an important part of customer service. As an administrator, your job is to check that your own customers have what they need *or* – if you couldn't meet a request – that they still feel positive about your organisation or your team.

Informal checks

These include:

- asking a caller if they have everything they need
- checking a caller understood what you have said
- asking if there is anything else you can do for them.

More formal checks:

These include:

- contacting a customer after you have done a job to find out if it was satisfactory
- contacting a customer after you have provided information to check it was complete and met their needs.

Dealing with complaints

If a customer is dissatisfied you want to find out quickly and take action. Most people are reasonable. If you were supposed to make 20 photocopies and misread this and only made two, then you can hardly expect your customer to be happy! You must then apologise and complete the job properly.

Occasionally you may feel a complaint is unjust. If you couldn't read the writing on a form, or you could swear the person asked for two copies, then you may feel like arguing! This is seldom advisable.

Sometimes, however, you may have to deal with a serious complaint which has nothing to do with you. This may be a complaint from a senior manager relating to your team, or a complaint from an external customer about the quality of your service or product. You are unlikely to be expected to deal with solving the problem – just deal with the customer. Do this by:

- listening carefully
- apologising to the customer for the inconvenience
- not putting the blame on anyone (or accepting the blame)
- noting down the details
- either asking a team member to deal with the person or – if the complaint is made by phone – arranging for someone to call back promptly.

Evidence collection

1   Keep a log of your customer requests over a period of a week or month. Your log must include providing *both* of the following services for *either* internal *or* external customers:

  ● taking and passing on messages
  ● providing administrative support (such as typing or photocopying).

The following headings are a useful guide.

Date	Name of customer	Internal/external customer	Service requested	Service provided	Deadline

2   Write a brief account which explains:

  a   the type of questions you ask customers if you are not sure what they want

  b   how you check you are giving the customer accurate and up-to-date information

  c   the type of information you are not allowed to provide

  d   why you think it is important to provide a service within an agreed timescale

  e   what checks you make to ensure your customers are satisfied with the service you provide – and what you do if they are not.

Ask your team leader or supervisor to countersign this for you.

3   If you record customer requests on a form, ask for a copy of these for your portfolio. Otherwise keep a copy of any notes you make when you receive such a request. These are invaluable evidence, particularly if you write a brief explanatory note about them before you file them as evidence.

4   If you have to deal with any problems or if you receive any complaints, write a brief description stating what happened and what you did. Ask the person to whom you reported the problem to counter-sign your description to confirm it.

Unit 107   Distribute and dispatch mail

> This unit is one of two Optional Group B units. You nee~~d~~
> this unit *or* unit 106 to gain your award, but not both.

This unit is concerned with the way:

- you receive, sort and distribute mail
- in which you dispatch mail.

It is **important** because:

- all organisations receive mail every day
- incoming mail must be processed and distributed promptly as it often contains important items which must be dealt with quickly
- outgoing and external mail must also be processed and dispatched promptly
- understanding how to process incoming and outgoing mail is an important skill for administrators to learn.

This unit comprises two elements. Before you start, you need to understand why handling mail efficiently is so important to organisations and the type of procedures that exist to ensure this is done.

Key skills signpost

If you are studying your key skills award in Communication at level 1 then you can extend your mail handling skills and obtain evidence for your key skills portfolio through your work for this unit.

Special note: You will need to do activity C2.2 *before* you do C2.1a or C1.2b.

C2.1a   You work for a small company and mail handling has always been carried out in one area in a general office. The new sales manager wants to start sending out far more computerised mail shots and has agreed that it will be necessary to have a proper mail handling room to cope with increased mail. He has asked for your suggestions as to how this should be set out and the equipment that may be needed. Find out as much as you can about this (see C2.2) and, in a small group of 3 or 4, discuss your ideas and decide on your suggestions. Keep your own notes safely as you will need these for C2.3.

C2.1b   Your tutor will take the role of your supervisor for this discussion. You have been asked to investigate the different ways in which mail can be sent quickly and to find out the different costs. Meet your tutor to present your ideas and discuss which would be the best for your own organisation.

C2.2 Check through the content of this unit in this book and make notes which you think will help you in your discussions for C2.1a. Add to this by researching additional information on mailrooms – either through the books in your library or by investigating the range of mailroom equipment available from major suppliers. If you have Internet access, useful sites to try are listed on page 212.

Find out the range of services available for sending mail quickly, from this book, from the Royal Mail (either obtain a leaflet from your post office or visit the Royal Mail website on www.royalmail.com) and from local couriers (check *Yellow Pages*). Use the information you obtain to inform your discussion in C2.1b.

After you have completed each of your discussions, write a brief summary about how the notes you made helped you in each case.

C2.3 **a** After you have completed your discussions for C2.1a, write a brief report which summarises your suggestions. You must include *one* image. This could be a drawing or sketch of the new mailroom with its equipment or a chart or table listing the items and identifying the approximate cost.

b After you have completed your discussions for C2.1b, write a memo to your tutor confirming what was agreed.

Distribute and dispatch mail

If you handle mail, you will handle both **incoming** and **outgoing** mail. You will also handle both **internal** and **external** mail. It is important that you understand the difference between all these terms.

- **Incoming mail** is that which is received by your organisation. Mostly it will contain external items received through the Royal Mail service but there will also be internal mail as well.
- **Outgoing mail** is that which is being sent out by your organisation, usually by the Royal Mail service.
- **Internal mail** is that which is received from other parts of your organisation (including branch offices) or which is being sent to them.
- **External mail** is that which is received from other organisations or individuals, or which is being sent to them.

Procedures for receiving and dispatching mail

All organisations have recommended ways or procedures for receiving and dispatching both internal and external mail. Often this will be in the form of a list, such as numbered points. You need to:

- know the procedures you must follow
- understand these and how they affect your job
- follow them!

If you learn mail handling in one organisation it is usually very easy to adapt your skills if you ever change your job.

Procedures for receiving mail

These are likely to include:

- the time by which mail usually must be sorted and distributed
- instructions as to whether mailroom staff open the mail or send the mail to individual departments unopened
- the methods used to record incoming mail items, if this is done in the mailroom
- how to prioritise incoming mail items
- how to deal with urgent or confidential items
- how to deal with suspicious or damaged items
- how to direct mail to the correct person
- how to report delays in opening and distributing mail.

You will learn general points about all these topics in this unit. However, different organisations will have their own slightly different procedures.

Procedures for dispatching mail

These are likely to include:

- whether outgoing mail will be collected from offices by mailroom staff – or whether office staff must deliver it to the mailroom
- the latest time by which outgoing mail must be received in the mailroom for processing that day
- the way in which internal mail to other offices is handled
- the normal postage put on routine items (usually second class)
- the action to take if a large mailshot is being sent
- organisational rules on personal mail
- any other organisational restrictions which relate to the cost of postage and the use of different services.

These topics are slightly different to those you will study in this unit – which are more concerned with how to *process* items of outgoing mail. For that reason, an extract from organisational procedures on outgoing mail is illustrated below, to show you the type of procedures you can expect to find in operation.

OUTGOING MAIL PROCEDURES

1 All normal mail must be received in the mailroom by 2.30 pm for dispatch the same day.

2 Large parcels, for packing and dispatch by mailroom staff that day, must be received no later than 1.30 pm.

3 The mailroom must be given at least 48 hours notice for very large numbers of items (e.g. mailshots).

4 All internal mail *must* be placed in the blue trays and all external mail in the red trays.

5 Items to be sent by special services, e.g. special delivery, registered post or recorded delivery – or those for which a certificate of posting is required – must be clearly marked.

6 All items will be sent by second-class postage unless marked otherwise.

7 All pre-stamped and Freepost items must be kept separate and put in the basket provided.

8 Personal mail will only be processed if it already has a stamp affixed.

9 All items must be placed in envelopes and securely sealed before being sent to the mailroom. It is the sender's responsibility to make sure the address is clearly legible and to check that all enclosures have been included.

10 Internal items may be placed in envelopes but will not be separately franked. Internal mail to branch offices will be dispatched in one large envelope to each branch office.

11 Staff with special, urgent items for dispatch or specific requests should contact the mailroom supervisor on extension 2398.

The importance of deadlines

Handling mail is often a highly pressurised job because it is constrained by strict time limits.

Incoming mail is normally delivered by the Royal Mail. If you work in a large organisation you may receive several sacks of mail and the time of delivery is likely to be early morning, maybe from 7.00 to 8.30 am. It is likely to be later if you work for a smaller firm which receives deliveries through the normal post system.

The first task of mailroom staff is to sort all the mail so that it can be distributed to staff as quickly as possible. In a very large organisation, the items may be left unopened – simply to save time. In a smaller one, everything except private and confidential items may be opened. The items then need processing and distributing to the correct people or departments.

This must happen fast because many people need to check their mail as soon as possible. They may be expecting an important document and need this before they can take further action about a matter. Sometimes the mail will contain unexpected information which may be critical to an action or decision. For all these reasons, it is normal for the mail to be delivered as quickly as possible.

Preparing **outgoing mail** for dispatch is just as pressurised because you only have a relatively short time between receiving it and meeting latest posting deadlines. Many large organisations have their mail collected by the Royal Mail service each day – and if the mail hasn't been processed by the time the collection is made, it has to be held over until the next day. If an item is important or urgent this can have serious repercussions – especially if the sender believes that the item was sent as promised.

Evidence collection

Find out what procedures exist in your organisation which affect the way in which mail is received and dispatched. Then highlight all those which are relevant to your own job, preferably giving examples of the tasks you do which relate to this part of the procedure.

Next identify the deadlines you have to work to. Do this by stating what time you start to open or sort incoming mail and the time by which it must be distributed to staff. Then state what time outgoing mail must be collected or received in the mailroom and the final deadline you have for posting it (or for the collection to be made).

Receive, sort and distribute mail

Imagine you work for an organisation with five departments – sales, finance, personnel, administration and production – each headed by a Director. Each department employs between 10 and 30 members of staff. In charge of everyone is the Managing Director who also has a Personal

Assistant (PA). Today is your first day in the mailroom and you are looking at seven sacks of mail. Some envelopes are addressed to individuals, others just to the organisation. At one side are a number of parcels. Some are marked 'urgent'. What do you do? Where do you start?

In this situation you would be one member of a team of people. It is only in a much smaller organisation, with far fewer employees (and much less mail), that you would be expected to learn how to do the job on your own.

DEALING WITH INCOMING MAIL

Receive mail
↓
Sort the mail into priority categories
↓
Open mail using mail-opening machine *except* for private and personal items
↓
Date stamp items and check enclosures are firmly attached
↓
Record specific items as requested (e.g. money received)
↓
Sort mail into departments
↓
Place mail into departmental baskets
↓
Put mail in baskets in priority order, i.e.
– private or personal on the top (unopened)
– next urgent items
– then first-class items
– then second-class, routine items
– finally, magazines, brochures and circulars

Information update

All mailrooms need appropriate equipment for processing incoming mail. The most basic is a desk, a letter-opening knife and a date stamp. In a larger organisation you can expect more mechanised equipment, more space, and trays or baskets for the incoming mail. You can therefore expect to find:

● a clear working area on which you can stack and open envelopes

- an electric letter opener which takes a tiny slice from the top of each envelope that passes through it. This minimises the danger of damaging the contents
- a container for empty envelopes. These are normally saved for a day in case there is a query about a missing enclosure
- a date stamp. This is used to identify the date when the item was received. It is useful for staff dealing with a matter if there has been a delay and there is a considerable difference between the date a document was sent and the date when it was received
- trays or baskets clearly marked with the names of different sections, offices or departments.

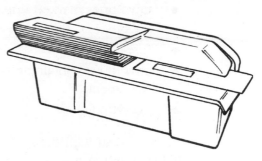

An electric letter opener can open up to 400 envelopes per minute

The layout of a mailroom needs to be organised carefully

Sorting and recording incoming mail

In a large organisation you may be instructed not to open the envelopes but simply to read them and put the items into the correct departmental basket. However, this is unusual. Most employers will expect you to do all the tasks listed in the box on page 208.

Sorting the mail into categories

This is done because, if there was a huge delivery one day and time was running short, only non-urgent, very routine items would then be left over until the next day.

It also helps that the Royal Mail service separates special items such as Special Delivery or Recorded Delivery as these must be signed for. You therefore know these are important and should deal with them first.

The main categories are as follows:
- special items (as above)

- envelopes marked urgent or important
- envelopes marked personal, or private and confidential
- first-class mail
- envelopes containing special enclosures, such as money or legal documents
- everything else!

How to deal with these is shown in the chart below. Items with your address but an unknown name should be reposted with 'not known at this address' written on the envelope. If you recognise the name, you could put a forwarding address on the envelope, if you know it. If both the name and address are wrong the item has been delivered to you in error. In all these cases you should repost the envelope, unopened. This costs nothing.

SORTING MAIL INTO PRIORITY ORDER	
Special items (e.g. Special Delivery)	– Sign for these on delivery. Open them first. Check to see if these must be recorded in an 'incoming mail log'.
Urgent and important items	– Open these and make sure they are kept separate in a priority pile. You may have to stamp these separately with a special stamp.
Personal or private and confidential items	– *Never* open. If you know the person is absent report the matter to your supervisor or team leader.
First-class mail	– Open these items and check the enclosures are firmly attached. Staple them if necessary.
Special enclosures	– Special enclosures include money (e.g. cheques) or legal documents. In many organisations these are recorded separately in an incoming mail log.
Everything else	– Open second-class, routine items. Sometimes these will be magazines or brochures which may need to be seen by several people. The usual method is to attach a circulation slip listing all the departments and send it to the first on the list.

Recording mail

Some organisations, such as special security establishments, record absolutely everything that is received. However, this takes a lot of time. Most organisations only record special items – and some record none at all in the mailroom. You will have to check the procedures where you work.

If you have to keep a record, this will usually be for special or valuable items in case there is a query later.

A **remittance book** was commonly used to record all monetary payments made by post. Today a record may be kept in the finance department or on computer in the mailroom. The type of headings you might see are shown below.

Date	Name	Amount received	Account No.	Comments
10 May	J Baxter	£210.50	09389	Cheque unsigned
	T Ashton	£45.60	18927	–
	J Allan	£1008.00	19872	–
	T Worthington	£657.00	03727	Cheque torn on opening

A remittance log

Suspicious or damaged items

Damaged items

If you look back at the items recorded above, you will see that one cheque was noted as being torn. This can happen accidentally when you are opening the mail – especially if you try to open it manually rather than using a letter opener or letter opening machine. Sometimes, of course, items are damaged in transit. You will identify this quickly because the Royal Mail service usually delivers such items in a transparent plastic bag explaining the problem.

Do make sure you report promptly any damage to items you are opening. If you accidentally damage something it is better to admit it.

Suspicious items

A suspicious item is something which looks strange or unusual, feels different or smells odd. You may think it is very dramatic to worry about mail bombs if you work for a small local organisation but, unfortunately, no matter where you work there is no guarantee that you will never receive anything suspicious in the mail. Organisations which are very concerned about mail security can buy special devices to scan mail. These will sound an alarm if any suspicious items are detected.

Treat an item as suspicious if:

- it is unusually heavy for its size
- the address is odd or the writing is peculiar
- you don't recognise the postmark
- it has far more stamps on it than necessary
- it smells of marzipan or almonds
- you can see wiring or tin foil if the package is damaged
- you can see grease marks on the envelope or wrapping.

At this point you *must* stop trying to open it, leave the package on the table, and inform your supervisor.

If you can't find your supervisor immediately then lock the door and, if you are completely on your own, dial 999 and tell the police about your worries.

Whatever you do, don't return to the room, be tempted to touch the package or use the telephone in that particular room – as this can trigger some devices.

If, afterwards, it was a false alarm, ignore anyone who thinks you were making a fuss about nothing or teases you. Think about the consequences if it had been a real threat and you had decided to carry on opening it. Which is worse?

Check it out!

If you have Internet access, then you can investigate the types of equipment and furniture required in a well-equipped mailroom quite easily. In addition you can find out about *outgoing* mail equipment and other accessories, such as trolleys for distributing large amounts of mail around an office block.

Each of the following are useful sites to explore:

- www.mailing-solutions.cossaxbiz.com
- www.neopost.co.uk
- www.fpmailing.co.uk
- www.northernservices.co.uk

A mail trolley can carry up to 60 kg of mail

Urgent and confidential mail

Remember that urgent and confidential items can be delivered at any time of the day by courier or by hand from a local organisation. This does not mean they should wait until the mailroom swings into operation the following day!

Remember, too, that if you sign for an item then you are the person who is listed as receiving it and it is therefore your responsibility to make sure it reaches the addressee as soon as possible.

If you are asked to sign for a parcel, and it is not your job to open it then read what you are signing. You do not want to sign that the contents are correct if you cannot check them. They may well be damaged! In this case, against your signature write 'contents not checked'. If the item is obviously damaged, then sign 'contents damaged on receipt' on the form – or check with your supervisor if you should refuse to accept the parcel.

Directing mail to the correct person

Mail can be delivered to the wrong person because:
- of a careless mistake
- of confusion over people or departments
- there is no name on the item being delivered.

Careless mistakes

Careless mistakes happen when someone scoops up a pile of mail for different people, originally in separate smaller piles, and confuses the start and end of each of these. When these are delivered to people's desks – or placed in people's mail trays – some items are wrongly delivered.

Although members of staff will quickly realise that two or three items are for someone else this does not mean they necessarily send them on immediately. On a busy day, they may simply put this in their out tray for re-delivery – which will cause a day's delay. It is unlikely that the member of staff will be prepared to walk the building to re-deliver it personally! The worst consequence is when the person who receives the item by mistake is out of the office for a few days. The item then simply sits in their in-tray – whilst the true recipient still anxiously awaits its arrival.

The best way is to do a double check when you actually deliver mail to people – or put it in their mail tray – to make sure that all the items are for that particular person.

Name confusion

You will learn to love people who address envelopes properly with the correct title, initial, name, job title and department! This means there is no confusion.

You will also like people with unusual names – because it is obvious that an item is for them – and get annoyed if there are five people called Patel or four called Smith working in your company, none of whom ever seems to tell anyone their initial(s) or job title!

There are two tips to minimise confusion and wrong delivery.

● Open the envelope and read the contents (providing you are allowed to do this). As you get to know your job and your organisation then you will become more skilled at seeing who is the best person to receive each item. If J. Patel works in finance and S. Patel works in personnel, then an invoice will go to J. Patel but a job application to S. Patel.

● Hedge your bets! If you are not sure whether J. Patel or S. Patel should receive an invoice for a training course, choose one and put a post-it note on the item asking this person to send it to the other if necessary.

Poorly addressed envelopes

Some envelopes – especially those containing 'junk mail' – may just show the name of the organisation. Others may have an unknown name – or the name of an employee who left last month or last year!

Other envelope problems include unreadable written names and those showing names which don't belong to anyone who works for your organisation.

In a small firm there may be one member of staff who is happy to receive these and forward them on for you to the best person. In a large organisation you can't do this. Again, use the contents to give you a clue as to the best department to deal with the matter. If you are still undecided, ask your mailroom supervisor for help.

Reporting delays

Again the procedure to follow will depend upon the size of your organisation.

● In a large organisation, if there is a problem, talk to the mailroom supervisor *before* it gets serious – not when there is a crisis. For instance, if the Royal Mail delivery was delayed for some reason, or two people in your team are off sick, you can't be expected to process the mail as quickly as normal.

Giving the supervisor plenty of notice means that he or she has the opportunity to obtain extra help or take other steps to remedy the problem .

- In a small firm, tell your team leader or line manager. Expect to be asked *why* the problem has occurred. Again, this could be anything from a late delivery to an unexpectedly large delivery. In the case of the latter, you may be instructed to deal with the urgent and first class items immediately and distribute these, and then do the rest. Again, giving plenty of warning enables your manager or team leader to make an appropriate decision in good time.

In both cases, expect to give reasons why there is a delay and an estimated time when the mail will be delivered. A word of warning: always slightly over-estimate this rather than under-estimate it – otherwise you may have to admit that you have missed yet another deadline because you didn't allow yourself enough time!

Evidence collection

1   Write a brief account which clearly states:

- the procedures you must follow when you receive and sort incoming mail
- how you handle and deliver incoming mail to make sure it goes to the right person as soon as possible
- to whom you would report any delays in mail distribution if you had a problem. If you have had this experience, state what happened, why it occurred and what you did about it at the time.

Ask your mailroom supervisor or line manager to countersign this to confirm it is true.

2   Keep a log of the items you receive, sort and distribute over a specific period, such as a week or month. Do make sure that your log includes items that:

- are both letters *and* parcels
- include both internal and external items of mail (i.e. items received from inside and outside the organisation).

Ask your mailroom supervisor or line manager to counter-sign your log to confirm it is accurate.

3   If you have ever received a damaged or suspicious item then state what you did at the time – and ask your mailroom supervisor or line manager to confirm this. If you have not, then expect your assessor to discuss this with you to find out what you would do, if this happened.

Dispatch mail

Procedures for handling outgoing mail will vary depending upon the size of the organisation, for instance:

- a large organisation may insist all mail items are packed or sealed within each department – the mailroom then simply prepares these for posting
- in a smaller organisation, you may receive some items in envelopes but others you will have to check and seal yourself.

In this element, you will learn the procedures to follow assuming you have to do everything – just in case you need to know this.

Preparing mail for dispatch

Throughout the day items for dispatch are received in the mailroom. These may include:

- parcels
- valuable items or important documents
- items for sending abroad
- routine external items
- routine internal items.

The mailroom staff then have to undertake a series of activities to prepare the mail for collection (or taking to the post) by a specified time. The normal sequence for external items is shown below.

Internal mail is normally placed direct into trays for distribution to offices or departments, or it may be placed into special pouches or wallets

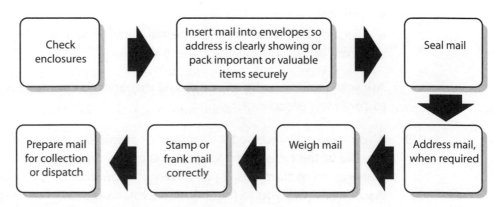

Sequence of activities for processing outgoing mail

which are easily readdressed and reusable many times. If you work for an organisation which has branch offices, then normally one large envelope or special pouch is prepared for each office and all the items for that destination are placed in it throughout the day. At the end of the day the envelope or pouch is sealed and franked (see page 223).

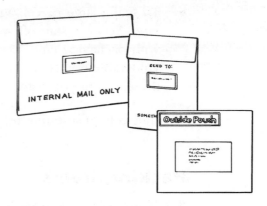

Pouches or wallets for internal mail

Checking mail and missing items

The first stage, when you receive an item for dispatch, is to check that you have everything you need to send. This is easy if you are posting one letter in an envelope. It is more difficult if you are making up a package of six booklets, three leaflets and a compliment slip.

A brief glance at outgoing letters should indicate if there should be enclosures if your organisation uses a system of typing Enc (for one) or Encs (for more than one) for enclosure at the bottom of the document. On other types of documents, a list of the enclosures may be typed at the bottom, which is even better – as then you can check them off one by one.

If you have been asked to pack a parcel, make sure you double check exactly what it must contain before you start – and make sure you have everything you need. If an item is missing, check who asked you to send this item and contact them immediately. If you don't know, refer the query to your mailroom supervisor or line manager.

Sealing mail

Most envelopes today are self-seal. Do be careful if you are inserting documents into a window envelope and make sure you fold them correctly so that *every* line of the address is showing clearly. To seal a jiffy bag or large parcel you need the right equipment and materials.

- The easiest way to seal a jiffy bag is to fold over the flap of the envelope and staple it together. Then cover the staples (both sides) with packaging tape. This is stronger and wider than sellotape.

- To seal a large parcel, again you should use strong, wide packaging tape. You can start off with sellotape, if you wish, but do cover it with packaging tape. Check that all joints, corners and other vulnerable points are protected – you can put packaging tape over these, too, if you want.

The aim is to ensure that no package you send disintegrates in the post!

Packing items

Jiffy bags are excellent for items which will fit in an envelope and need padded protection – such as floppy disks, for instance – or for heavy items such as a book. Cardboard-backed envelopes are available for items such as certificates and photographs. These are clearly marked 'Do not bend' on the front.

However, you cannot use a jiffy bag or cardboard-backed envelope to send a fragile vase or a photograph in a glass frame through the post. In this case something more substantial is required.

A variety of packaging materials are on the market, including bubble wrap and polystyrene shapes or balls. A cheaper alternative is all the bits out of the office shredder – because these are free! So is old newspaper!

You basically need to use the packaging materials in two ways:

1   The first step is to protect the item. Bubble wrap is ideal – simply wrap it tightly around the item several times and sellotape it.

2   The second step is to make sure there is no spare space in the box you are using for the item to bump about. You can fill this with polystyrene shapes, paper waste from the shredder *or* tear some newspaper yourself (preferably into long strips). Make sure you put plenty of material around the item, so all the space is taken up.

Bubble wrap is ideal for protecting fragile items

Then fasten the box and seal it. Next, stick a 'fragile' sticker on the top and sides. Finally, if necessary, label the box 'this way up' with an arrow.

Addressing mail

If you deal with incoming mail, you know how important it is that mail is addressed correctly. The Royal Mail also like clear, well addressed envelopes, packages and parcels.

If you use a word processing package, then you will obviously produce an easy-to-read envelope. On most software packages it will also be automatically positioned in the right place. However, sometimes you will have to handwrite a label or an address on a parcel. You need to:

- write *very* clearly
- use a water-resistant pen (such as a biro, not a roller ball)
- follow all the rules in the chart below.

ENVELOPE ADDRESSING

Rules to follow

- Start an envelope half way down and one third of the way across. (So you start the address in a central position on the envelope.)
- Start each line vertically under the previous line.
- Write the name of the addressee and his/her title (e.g. Mr J Brown).
- If you are writing to a business contact, next write the job title (e.g. Sales Manager) and then the name of the firm.
- Start a new line for each line of the address
- Always write the name of the town in CAPITALS
- *Don't* use abbreviations – such as Rd for Road or St for Street. However, there are some allowable abbreviations for long county names, e.g. Glos for Gloucestershire.
- The postcode must be the last item, preferably on a separate line. It must not contain *any* punctuation or be underlined.
- If you are addressing an envelope to go abroad, put *both* the city (or town) *and* the country name in capitals. Don't be surprised if the address is in a strange order – in some countries the town is shown before the street or the number of the house after the street name.
- Write any special mailing instructions in capitals at the top left, e.g. AIRMAIL or URGENT.
- If the item must be marked PERSONAL (or Private and Confidential) then this is written two lines *above* the name line.
- If you are sending a package or parcel you must put the sender's name (i.e. your organisation) and address on the reverse side.

Test your knowledge and understanding

1   Write three envelopes, one for each of the following addressees. Ask your tutor or supervisor to check them for accuracy:

   a   Mrs Julie Shepherd, 14 Highbury Road, Blackpool, Lancs, BL5 3WK

   b   Mr K O'Reilly, Distribution Manager, Fawkes and Cox plc, 15 Foyle Road, Coleraine, County Londonderry, Northern Ireland BT52 2PD

   c   Mr D Wilkins, 15 Beveridge Drive, Newmarket, Ontario, L3Y 9Y3, Canada

2   How many mistakes can you spot in the following envelope? You should find eight! Check your ideas with the key on page 227.

PERSONAL

Nicky Escreet
    15 Juniper Rd
    EDGEHILL
    Liverpool
    <u>L20 9JF.</u>

Postage charges

The cost of sending something depends upon three factors:

- the weight
- the destination
- any special services required.

The weight

Most people are familiar with the cost of sending a standard letter by first class or second class post. However, this does not mean that you can put 10 sheets of paper and a booklet in an envelope and expect it to cost the same as one sheet of paper! There is a weight limit of 60 grams and beyond that the price increases.

The destination

If you are sending your letter or package abroad you have to consider other factors. For pricing, the world is divided into three areas: Europe, World Zone 1 and World Zone 2.

Each has different prices and, again, it depends upon the weight.

The service

You may want something more than basic first class or second class mail. You may want your item to get there quickly. Or, if it is valuable, you may want to take out additional protection. These type of services will cost you more.

If the item is *very* urgent you may want to pay a courier to take it. You can often see courier bikes speeding around large towns and cities or see adverts for large distribution companies such as DHL on television. This type of service is quite costly but worth it if the item must arrive safely by a specific time.

Information update

If you see the name Consignia plc on something relating to the mail, don't be alarmed! This is the new name which has been adopted by the Royal Mail, Parcelforce and Post Office. This has been done to help British mail services compete more easily abroad as the name is felt to be more easily recognised and remembered.

Check it out!

Visit your local Post Office and obtain some leaflets on the type of services that are available. Alternatively, visit royalmail.com and find out about the services on the Internet. Then do the quiz below. (A key is given on page 227.)

1 The **free** service which enables you to obtain confirmation you have posted something is:

    a Recorded delivery

    b Special delivery

    c Certificate of posting.

2 The service used to send normal items quickly overseas is:

    a Special delivery

    b Certificate of posting

    c Airmail.

3 The service used to spend special items very quickly overseas is:

    a Swiftair

    b Recorded delivery

    c Airmail.

4 The service used to send valuable documents (such as a certificate or legal contract) to someone in the UK is:

    a Airmail

    b Recorded delivery

    c Certificate of posting.

5 The service used to send items very quickly in the UK (you get a refund if they are not delivered by 12 noon the following day) is:

    a Airmail

    b Swiftair

    c Special delivery.

Calculating postage charges

In most mailrooms today you will find electronic scales which automatically calculate the correct postage charge. You simply put the item on the scales, key in any special services or special destination and the correct charge is shown on the display.

It is worth remembering two points:

- make sure you place the envelope or packet centrally on the scale so it is not leaning on anything
- check that you press the correct keys for any special services or destination!

Note that many of these scales can only take envelopes or small packets. If you are weighing a large parcel, you will have to use special parcel scales which take heavier weights. If these only give you the weight – not the charge – you then have to read off the charge on a postage rate chart. Do check that you have done this correctly with a more experienced colleague until you are certain you can do it accurately on your own.

Digital weighing scales

Franking machines

Many business organisations use franking machines. These have several advantages:

- franking machines operate very quickly, so outgoing mail is processed much faster
- there is no need to keep a supply of stamps in the mailroom
- the machine prints the exact amount of the postage on the envelope
- labels can be printed for sticking on parcels and packets

Franking machines have many advantages

- as well as the postage amount, adverts and slogans can be added, as well as a return address for undelivered mail.

A variety of models is available – so the type you use (and its speed) will vary depending upon how much mail you usually send each day. A large organisation is more likely to have a bigger and faster machine than a small firm.

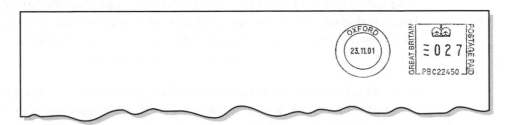

A franked label

The system works because postage units are stored in the machine. When these run out they can be topped up easily. Authorised staff make a telephone call to the manufacturer and the additional units can be transferred into the machine electronically.

Information update

Believe it or not, only 10% of businesses actually use a franking machine. This is because many use stamps as they are cheaper than buying or leasing a franking machine. The good news is that self-adhesive stamps at least don't need licking!

Using a franking machine

All franking machines are sold with a handbook and it is sensible to read this and to watch a demonstration before you try it out yourself.

The process is normally quite automated.

- Depending upon the design of the machine, you may place the envelopes in a hopper or feeder tray – but must make sure these are the right way up and facing in the right direction. Otherwise you might frank the wrong side or the bottom, not the top!
- Check the postage is set correctly (first or second class post).
- Check the date is correct (this is normally automatically changed on modern machines).
- Set the machine in operation.
- The envelopes pass through the machine to a receiving tray.

Warning

If you realise you have made a mistake, don't try to interfere with the process. Learn how to stop the machine quickly – or remove further envelopes from the feeder tray. Tell your supervisor if you have overfranked or underfranked items in error. Don't panic and try to hide the envelopes.

If the image is faint then tell your supervisor. This is important as the Royal Mail may refuse to handle items if the postage rate is not clear. Some machines automatically inform you (on a display) if the postage is running low. Again, tell your supervisor.

If your mail is not collected and you take franked mail to the post box you must *never* just post it as ordinary mail. Franked mail goes in a special envelope and, in some districts, in a specially marked postbox.

Information update

If you are very fortunate you may work in a fully automated mailroom where the electronic scales are linked to the franking machine or the franking machine will do both operations so that it not only calculates the weight but franks the item as well!

In some mailrooms for large organisations there are also machines which automatically fold and insert documents.

Some mailrooms will have a folder-inserter machine

Sending mail out on time

There are a number of reasons why outgoing mail may be delayed *occasionally*, for example:

- there is an unusually large number of items for some reason
- some members of the mailroom staff are absent
- some mail is delivered late
- a problem with the franking machine or other equipment.

Because it is important to meet postal deadlines with the majority of mail, you must inform your supervisor or line manager if you think there is a problem, so that the correct decision can be made. This will usually be to concentrate on dispatching all urgent and first-class items and to leave routine items (such as mailshots and invoices) until the following day.

However, never second guess what your supervisor might decide to do! State the reason for the delay calmly and try to make positive suggestions as to how the bulk of the important items can be dealt with that day.

Evidence collection

You must prove that you dispatch:

- both letters *and* parcels
- items which are being sent outside your organisation *and* items which are being sent to destinations inside your organisation.

1   Write a brief account for your assessor which explains:

   a   the procedures you must follow when you are dispatching mail

   b   the checks you make to ensure the mail contains all the correct items

   c   how you seal mail to make sure it is secure and safe from damage

   d   how you address mail

   e   the system you use to make sure mail is stamped or franked correctly

   f   what you do if you have a problem dispatching mail on time.

2   Keep a log of the items you dispatch over a period of a week or month (depending upon how many items you process every day) until you have listed about 30 items. A useful set of headings is shown below.

Date	Item	Weight	Destination

Ask your mailroom supervisor or line manager to countersign this to confirm it is correct.

3   State how you deal with internal mail and state what you do that is different when you are handling items for internal distribution and items which have to be sent outside the organisation.

Keys to quizzes

Unit 102: Key to quiz on page 74

a Refer the matter to your supervisor. Check the manual to find out the correct action to take. Don't be tempted to wedge it shut or lean on it, if the manual clearly says the machine should never be operated with the door open.

b Look to see if any long poles are available. Contact the caretaker to see if he/she can help. Open the door in the meantime.

c Ring the electricians (or your safety officer) and explain what happened. Draw up a list of all the electrical equipment in the office so that this won't happen again.

d Make her take a break and have a cup of tea or coffee. Say it is important she talks to your team leader about the problem or she will make herself ill. If it will help, volunteer to speak to the team leader yourself.

e If the leaflet is available, check the correct action to take. If not, wash it off immediately. Start with plenty of cold water. Then find a leaflet and make sure there is no other action you should take.

f The fuse has 'blown'. Try replacing the fuse (check the correct amp to use). If it 'pops' again, don't use it. Put a label on that it is faulty and notify your supervisor or in-house electrician.

Unit 102: Key to quiz on page 76

1 a, 2 b, 3 c, 4 b, 5 c, 6 a, 7 c.

Unit 103: Key to envelope on page 117.

1 False, 2 True, 3 False, 4 True, 5 False, 6 False, 7 False, 8 True, 9 True, 10 True.

Unit 107: Key to envelope on page 220.

1 Personal should be written two spaces above the name.
2 There is no title (Miss, Mrs, Ms).
3 The first line doesn't line up with the rest.
4 The writing starts too high up.
5 Road should be written in full.
6 Edgehill is the district but Liverpool is the city and this should be in capitals – not Edgehill.
7 The postcode should not have a full stop at the end.
8 The postcode should not be underlined.

Unit 107: Key to postal services quiz on page 222.

1	**c**	Certificate of posting	**4**	**b**	Recorded delivery
2	**c**	Airmail	**5**	**c**	Special delivery
3	**a**	Swiftair			

Appendix: Developing yourself

This final section concentrates on applying for a job and improving your interview skills.

Applying for a job

If you have been studying your NVQ1 award at College, you may now be thinking about applying for a job. If you are already working, you will be unusual if you stay in the same job for life! In this case, you will want to use your new-found skills to help you to move on either in your current organisation or, at a later stage, to apply for jobs elsewhere.

Jobs in administration

Generally, you can expect to have:

- a more specialised job role in a large organisation. For instance, many firms employ data input clerks to input data into a database or a full-time receptionist to deal with visitors.
- a wider job role in a smaller organisation. In this case you may be expected to answer the telephone, do filing, use a computer, photocopy and deal with callers.

The NVQ Administration schemes have been specifically designed to give you the skills which employers need. Most are also very concerned that you have good IT skills and can deal with customers well because both these areas are considered very important. If you have additional skills in these areas – then say so!

Finding a vacancy

You may obtain information on a vacancy from:

- the Careers Service (now sometimes called Connextions) or the Job Centre
- your tutor or Student Services at college
- your local newspaper
- a local recruitment or employment agency.

Don't forget, too, that you may also have the opportunity to join a Modern Apprenticeship scheme. If you become a Foundation Modern Apprentice then you will study up to NVQ 2; if you become an Advanced Modern Apprentice then you will study up to NVQ 3.

In both these cases you will have a permanent job, but the vacancy will be suggested by a training agency or other organisation, who will send you for an interview. You will also be given time off from work to study for your NVQ. If you are interested in this option, talk to your tutor about opportunities in your area.

Check it out!

You need to read job advertisements very carefully to check that you can meet the minimum requirements which have been specified.

Check through your local newspaper and find *two* advertisements which would not be appropriate for you now, but would be if you were more skilled or experienced. Then think about how these help you to see which skills you should try to develop.

Try, too, to select one advertisement which would be suitable for you and discuss why you think this is the case with your tutor or trainer.

Making an application

Your careers adviser, tutor or the advertisement will tell you how you should make an application. You may have to complete an application form or you may have to send your CV (see next page) with a covering letter.

Application forms

Application forms are normally designed to be quite straightforward, but if you make a silly mistake you can spoil your chances immediately. It is therefore sensible to *photocopy* the form first, and practise on the photocopy. Ask someone to check what you have written before you write on the original form.

Golden rules include:

- reading the form all the way through before you start
- checking if you have to use a particular type of pen (black ink is often required)
- making sure you understand every question
- checking where you have to use block capitals.

Common mistakes include:

- putting the current year for your date of birth
- writing the postcode in the wrong place (check if it should be in the address part or in a separate part)
- scruffy or illegible handwriting

- spelling errors
- forgetting to sign and date the form at the end, if this is asked for.

The hardest part is the short, 'open' section on some forms where you may have to say why you think you are suitable for the job. Ask your tutor or trainer to help you with this. You need to focus on stating what you are good at and the areas where you have experience, for instance from working in a College office or in a part-time job. If you are good at IT and are studying for extra qualifications then say so!

Letters and CVs

The letters 'CV' stand for **curriculum vitae**. This is a summary sheet about you and your achievements to date. It *must* look professional, so you should create it on a word processor and only send an original document – not a photocopy.

Golden rules for a CV include:
- keeping it short – one A4 page is ideal
- setting it out clearly – use bold and different type sizes to make the headings stand out
- putting your personal information first
- listing your achievements in reverse chronological order – so that your most recent qualifications and experience are at the top
- concentrating on what you have done at work, college or in your final years at secondary school – anything before this is irrelevant
- asking your referees for their agreement *before* you include their names (either *or* on a CV *or* on an application form!).

Mistakes include:
- attaching a photograph – unless this is requested
- writing too much
- exaggerating your qualifications – *never* claim to have a qualification or a grade you haven't achieved
- exaggerating your skills or abilities.

It is usual to send your CV with a brief covering letter that explains why you are sending it. This letter must:
- include your home address
- be dated
- be addressed to the correct person
- include any reference numbers specified in the advertisement
- be easy to read – today it is quite acceptable to prepare the letter on a word processor *unless* the advertisement says otherwise
- be signed by you.

Test your knowledge and understanding

An example CV is shown below, together with a covering letter. Check through this, making sure you understand why all the headings have been used.

Now prepare your own CV. You can either use this layout or a different one suggested by your tutor.

Assume your local college has advertised for a trainee administrator in the Business Department. Write a covering letter to the Personnel Officer at the College, quoting the reference BD298.

REHANA PATEL

Address:	14 Barrowford Way, Hightown, HG6 3ML
Telephone:	01728 683737
Nationality:	British
Date of birth:	12 June 1984
Marital status:	Single

EDUCATION

2000–2001	Hightown College	Business with IT course
1995–2000	Westward High School	Studying for GCSEs

QUALIFICATIONS OBTAINED

June 2001	OCR	NVQ 1 Administration
June 2001	Edexcel	Key Skills level 1 in Numeracy, IT and Communications
June 2001	OCR	Text processing 1
June 2000	Southern Examining Board	GCSEs English Language (C) Business Studies (D) Maths (D) Geography (E)

QUALIFICATIONS TAKEN BUT RESULTS NOT YET KNOWN

June 2001	OCR	CLAIT (Computer literacy and Information Technology

WORK EXPERIENCE

March 2001	Hightown District Council	Administration work

ADDITIONAL INFORMATION

I have worked each weekend at Blockbuster video store in Hightown for the past two years and am used to helping and serving customers.
I am learning to drive.

REFEREES

Mrs J Brookes, Tutor, Hightown College, Newby Road, Hightown, HG1 3SL. Telephone 01728 - 382798
Mr T Harper, Manager, Blockbusters Video Store, Swan Street, Hightown, HG2 5KS. Telephone 01728 - 603982

```
                                                          14 Barrowford Way
                                                                   HIGHTOWN
                                                                    HG6 3ML

14 July 2001

Mrs Pat Winston
Chevers, Dunn and Parsley
Solicitors
10 Westgate
HIGHTOWN
HG3 2S0

Dear Mrs Winston

TRAINEE ADMINISTRATOR – REFERENCE TA12

I would like to be considered for the position of trainee administrator which was
advertised in the Hightown Gazette yesterday.

I have just completed a one year administration course at Hightown College
where I also studied IT. I am attaching my CV which gives full details of the
qualifications I have taken and my results to date.

I am very interested in legal work and would very much welcome the
opportunity to work for a well-known firm of solicitors such as yours.

I can attend for interview at any time.

Yours sincerely

Rehana Patel

Rehana Patel
```

Improving your interview skills

Very few people enjoy being interviewed. Most people are worried
that:

- they won't know what to say
- they won't be able to answer the questions
- they will talk too much, or not enough.

Preparing for an interview doesn't mean you won't be nervous. It
will, however, help you to feel more confident. This should mean that
you talk more easily and positively and give a better impression of
yourself.

Remember also that:

- an interview should be a two-way process – *you* should be finding out whether the job is suitable for you
- if you aren't successful
  - you can count the experience as good practice
  - remember that there are other jobs out there – this one just wasn't for you.

A word about tests

Your interview may include one or more tests.

- Keyboarding tests used to be quite common, but if you have a current keyboarding or word processing qualification then you are unlikely to be asked to do this.
- Psychometric tests are often used. It is almost automatic for you to be given one of these if you are applying to be a Modern Apprentice as this helps to determine your occupational area of interest and the best level for you to start on.

  In a psychometric test you are asked dozens of different questions. It is virtually impossible to lie because you can't remember your answers to earlier questions! Normally the areas covered include:
  - your verbal abilities
  - your numerical abilities
  - how well you can understand abstract concepts
  - your mechanical skills
  - how well you deal with other people
  - how you think
  - your coping skills.

  You should be very interested in the outcome of the test and ask for feedback. You don't want to know your scores – you want to know what these mean.

- Communication and numeracy tests are also given by some organisations. It depends upon the job you are applying for. If you have recently gained your Key Skills award at level 1, you may not be asked to do these – so there is an obvious benefit in getting the award!

Interview preparation

Before the interview

- Check the date, the day and the time carefully.
- Find out where the organisation is situated, how to get there and – most important – how much travelling time you will need to arrive in good time.

- Think about your appearance. Always be more conservative than normal. If you find out later that everyone wears jeans then that's fine – but these aren't interview clothes! Good guidelines are to choose clothes which:
  - are loose, rather than tight
  - are crease-resistant
  - are scrupulously clean (including your shoes!)
  - are neatly ironed
  - make you feel you look your best.
- You should also make sure your personal appearance is great – squeaky clean hair and clean nails are essential. If you are female, wear slightly less make-up than normal – not more!
- Find out about the organisation. How big it is? What does it do? Is it local or national? Have you read any of its advertisements?
- Think about the job and what type of skills you must stress you have. To help, list all the things you have done or experiences you have had which prove you work hard and have done well – or can do a good job. Remember to mention these during the interview.
- Think about the type of questions you may be asked.
  - Why did you decide to apply for this job?
  - What interests you about this job?
  - What subjects did you enjoy most at school/college?
  - Why do you want to work in administration?

  Bear in mind that if you have an odd gap in your CV or work history then your interviewer will want to explore this – so be ready with an explanation.
- Decide what to take with you to the interview, such as your Progress File or Record of Achievement, a reference from a part-time employer or examples of excellent work you have produced.
- Think about questions *you* can ask at the interview. Most interviewers invite you to ask questions so you should always have one or two ready. Avoid those which focus on how many holidays or pay rises you can expect to get! For example:
  - Will I be able to continue to develop my computer skills?
  - Will I be able to continue to study for NVQ awards?
  - What are the exact hours of work?
  - Will I be expected to work overtime?
  - If I worked hard, could you tell me what my promotion prospects might be?
  - I know that your organisation manufactures plastic products. Could you tell me what type of products you make?

At the interview

Give a good first impression

- Aim to arrive about 10 minutes early.
- Give your name to the receptionist and say why you are there. Remember to be polite and to smile (not grin!) Other staff may be asked what they thought about you later!
- When asked to meet the interviewer, take a deep breath and try to relax.
- Knock before you enter the room.
- If the interviewer holds out his/her hand, shake it firmly – so yours doesn't feel like a floppy rag!
- Don't sit down until you are invited to do so.
- If you are holding a folder or bag, don't clutch it to you like a shield. Put a bag on the floor, a folder on a desk or table.

Communicate positively with the interviewer

- Don't avoid eye contact – no matter how shy you are.
- *Never* smoke or chew during an interview. If you are a smoker, remember that most organisations have no smoking policies these days!
- Speak clearly. Avoid 'fillers' and ungrammatical sentences such as, 'Well, you know . . .' and 'er, um'.
- Look and sound interested and enthusiastic and keen to get the job. This is vital.
- Never answer just 'yes' or 'no' – give proper, full answers. *But* if you are apt to talk for too long, *don't*!
- Sit up straight, don't slouch and try to manage a smile when you can!
- Don't fiddle with your hair, bag or jewellery.
- Don't mention personal details or problems.
- Never be negative, e.g. 'I think filing is boring', 'I didn't like school', 'I hated college', 'I didn't like my last boss'.
- Don't argue or contradict the interviewer – no matter what you think!

Coping with problem areas

- If you don't understand a question say so politely, for instance, 'I'm sorry, I'm not sure I understand what you mean. Could you repeat the question again, please?'
- If you are asked what questions you would like to ask, remember your prepared list. If all these have already been asked, simply say, 'I did have some questions to ask but you've covered everything I wanted to know, thank you.'

- You may be asked a hypothetical question, such as, 'What would you do if you were alone on reception and the phone rings as a visitors appears?'. If you can, think about a previous similar situation when you have had to cope with this. Otherwise, simply use your common sense!

The final touches

Finally, remember that the interviewer is trying to assess not only your qualifications but also:

- how keen and eager you are to work hard and get on
- how well you will get on with the other people you will be working with
- how well you can express yourself and say what you mean.

Use the interview as an opportunity to prove this. Use your own experiences so far, such as any work experience you have done, any part-time job, voluntary work or additional activities – especially where you have worked in a team or with a group of other people. You have to sound as if you *enjoy* work and *really* want to work for that organisation, doing that job. It makes all the difference!

Zenith Communications

To: _____

From: _____

_____

Tel No: _____

☐ Please Ring Back   ☐ Will Ring Back

☐ Returned Your Call   ☐ URGENT

Message: _____

_____

_____

_____

_____

_____

_____

_____

_____

Date: _____ Time: _____ Taken By: _____

LEARNING PLAN

Name .... Date plan started ....

Employer's name or College ....

Name of reviewer .... Review date ....

Development aim	Target date	Activity	Outcome (✓ when achieved)

To be completed before the next review by employee or student
Identify any areas still outstanding. If these should have been completed by review date, give reasons for non-achievement.

Signed .... Date ....

PHOTOCOPIER RECORD

Your name ....

No. of originals	No. of copies required:	Other requirements (e.g. sorting and fastening copies):

Quality checks you made:

Methods you used to minimise waste paper:

Work undertaken satisfactorily ....Date ....

(This should be signed by the person who requested the work)

Remember to attach examples of your photocopying to this form

Index